D0908116

The Practice of Love

ASHLEY MONTAGU is a world-famous anthropologist and social biologist. He is the author of numerous books, including *The Direction of Human Development: Biological and Social Bases of Love; On Being Human; Prenatal Influences; Touching; Sex, Man, and Society;* and *Culture and Human Development* (Prentice-Hall, 1974).

Nor can that endure which has not its foundation upon love. For love alone diminishes not, but shines with its own light; makes an end of discord, softens the fires of hate, restores peace in the world, brings together the sundered, redresses wrongs, aids all and injures none; and who so invokes its aid will find peace and safety and have no fear of future ill.

—QUEEN LUDWIGA OF POLAND, 1413 A.D.

It is strange that men will talk of miracles, revelations, inspirations, and the like, as things past, while love remains.

—HENRY DAVID THOREAU

Edited by

ASHLEY MONTAGU

The
Practice of
Love

A SPECTRUM BOOK
PRENTICE-HALL, INC., Englewood Cliffs, New Jersey

Library of Congress Cataloging in Publication Data
MAIN ENTRY UNDER TITLE:

The Practice of love.

(A Spectrum Book)
Bibliography: p.
CONTENTS: Montagu, A. Introduction.—Chapman, G.
Valerio speaks of love.—Montagu, A. A scientist looks
at love. [etc.]
   1. Love—Addresses, essays, lectures. I. Montagu,
Ashley, date
BF575.L8P7   158'.2   75-14436
ISBN 0-13-694471-X
ISBN 0-13-694463-9 pbk.

© 1975 by Ashley Montagu. A SPECTRUM BOOK. All rights
reserved. No part of this book may be reproduced in any form or
by any means without permission in writing from the publisher.
Printed in the United States of America.

10 9 8 7 6 5 4 3 2 1

PRENTICE-HALL INTERNATIONAL, INC. (*London*)

PRENTICE-HALL OF AUSTRALIA PTY. LTD. (*Sydney*)

PRENTICE-HALL OF CANADA LTD. (*Toronto*)

PRENTICE-HALL OF INDIA PRIVATE LIMITED (*New Delhi*)

PRENTICE-HALL OF JAPAN, INC. (*Tokyo*)

PRENTICE-HALL OF SOUTHEAST ASIA (PTE.) LTD. (*Singapore*)

To the Memory of Ananda Coomaraswamy

Contents

The Practice of Love

Introduction

It is curious that while so much has been written on love by poets, playwrights, novelists, philosophers, and theologians, social and behavioral scientists should have paid so little attention to so important a subject. The mention of the word in such quarters still seems to cause the kind of embarrassment that the word "sex" used to produce, not so many years ago, in "respectable" circles. Most social and behavioral scientists still tend to shy away from the subject, although there have always been some outstanding exceptions. Here a representative number of some of these "exceptions"—anthropologists, sociologists, psychotherapists, psychologists, pediatricians, an educationist, and a philosopher—present their views on the subject of love.

The object of this book is to enable the reader to reevaluate his understanding of the meaning of love, and on the assumption that the meaning of a word is the action it produces, the title of the book, *The Practice of Love*, reflects the design to encourage the reader to put into practice the principles he acquires from the experience of the many authorities who, from their own particular angles of vision, have given us these new insights into the meaning of love.

We live in a time in which there is much talk of love, and much confusion concerning its meaning. Scarcely anyone can be found who can define it. Most people find the attempt intimidatingly difficult. And if it is true that what we know about anything is the way we behave about it, then it would appear that many of us do not know much above love. We confuse it with sex, with permissiveness, with "never having to say you're sorry," and so on. Words conceal our confusion. Yet it is not as important to be able to define a thing as to understand it. And truly to understand love means not so much what we do with the mind as what we accomplish with the heart. For love is not so much a thought as an act. We perceive every day about us the proof of the fact that it is quite possible to understand the meaning of love intellectually, and yet be quite unloving, while others who may have no intellectual comprehension of love may be remarkably good at the practice of it. Ask a baby's loving mother to define love, and whatever her actual words, her reply will be, "Child. Look into your heart and rejoice." *She* requires no definitions, no hornbook of instructions. Having been adequately loved in her own childhood, she knows how to love, for the only way one ever learns to love is by being loved. And once having been loved, one needs no further lessons. In human communication, which is the art of embracing the other, one does not need to be a grammarian—all one needs is a heart.

Beware of those who put ideas first, those "lovers" of humanity by the book, as Dostoyevsky called them. They put ideas before human beings, and in the name of some new shibboleth for humanity will abandon all humanity, and all morality in the name of morality. Let us be certain that those who draw up the blueprints for the future can feel as well as plan, love as well as think.

Those who have been inadequately loved, who need to learn how to love, and those who love well but have to deal with people who have been failed in this most important of all needs, both need to understand something of the nature of love—what it is, how it comes about, and how essential it is for healthy growth and development. This book is, therefore, designed to appeal to all kinds of readers: those who want to know what love is, those who want to improve themselves as loving human beings, and those who want to help others become lovers of their fellow human beings—and step by step, the whole of nature of which they are a part, for as a species we are an indissoluble part of nature, not the masters of it.

If as a species we are to survive, we must learn to live together not only with our fellow human beings but with the whole of nature. Otherwise our term on this earth which we have so much abused is perilously near its end. The faceless figures in the crowded landscape of abandoned humanity cry out for help, as does the animal world toward which we have been so mindlessly and heartlessly destructive. Rich or poor, educated or ignorant, the love of most people remains unexpressed and unexpressible. Caught up in the world in which scientific and technological progress has brought about spiritual anarchy, degradation, and decay, the concern of most people with things has become a substitute for affection, the affection they have neither the will nor the confidence to offer their fellow human beings. In such a world, people at best love as they must, not as they should. There is only too often an absence of love behind the show of love; few are able to distinguish the genuine from the spurious. Love becomes a commodity in the marketplace of exploitative human relationships. Sex becomes identified with love, and as a commodity love becomes a bargaining point conditional upon the fulfillment of the requirements demanded by the other. It is not surprising, therefore, that in the course of such transactions the essential unconditional quality of love is lost, that what passes for love is more often than not self-interest. "If you do as I wish I will love you. If you do not, then I will not love you."

Parents make their love conditional upon "good behavior." Children thus learn to grow up into people who use love to achieve their own selfish ends. In this way love is almost wholly conditioned out of existence, and a counterfeit marketing device is substituted for it. The "success" ethos further contributes to the debasement of the love motif. The built-in design for success becomes an instrument for the suppression of emotion and the denial of love. Business is pursued as a way of life rather than as a way of making a living, till the very purpose of becoming and being is lost.

And what is the purpose of becoming and being? As a student of man's evolutionary history, it is unequivocally clear to me that it is to live as if to live and love were one. It is a principal purpose of this book to make that point clear.

GEORGE CHAPMAN

Valerio Speaks of Love

George Chapman (1559–1634), friend and fellow actor of Shakespeare, friend and co-author of Ben Jonson, translator of Homer into English and by far the best of that ilk, the subject of Keats' famous sonnet, "On First Looking into Chapman's Homer," playwright, and poet, is the author of the finest description of the nature and the effects of love with which I am acquainted. This occurs in a speech made by Valerio, son of the knight Gostanzo, in Chapman's play, *All Fools*, written and performed in 1599. If Chapman had done nothing else, these lines would, in my view, have rendered him immortal, for no one has ever given so accurate and insightful a description of love as this. No behavioral scientist could ever say it in quite those words, but many have said it in rather crasser terms, invoking biochemistry, anatomy, endocrinology, ethology, and behavior, to mention only a few disciplines, to contribute their mite to the understanding of a human trait which most of them still tend to slight.

> I tell thee, Love is Nature's second Sun,
> Causing a spring of virtues where he shines;
> And as without the Sun, the World's great eye,
> All colours, beauties, both of Art and Nature,
> Are given in vain to men; so without Love
> All beauties bred in women are in vain,
> All virtues born in men lie buried;
> For Love informs them as the Sun doth colours;
> And as the Sun, reflecting his warm beams
> Against the earth, begets all fruits and flowers;
> So Love, fair shining in the inward man,
> Brings forth in him the honourable fruits
> Of Valour, wit, virtue, and haughty thoughts,
> Brave resolution: and divine discourse:
> Oh, 'tis the Paradise, the heaven of earth.
>
> *(All Fools,* Act I, sc. i)

ASHLEY MONTAGU

A Scientist Looks at Love

This essay may serve as a general introduction to the subject and the contributions that follow. It has not been usual for scientists to look at love, and it still isn't. All the more reason, therefore, for us to take a look at what scientific inquiry has been able to reveal about the dynamics of love.

The study of love is something from which scientists, until very recently, have shied away. With the increase, however, of interest in the origins of mental illness in this century, more and more attention has begun to be paid to the infancy and childhood of human beings. What has been revealed by these investigations is that love is, without any question, the most important experience in the life of a human being.

What is love? One of the most frequently used words in our vocabulary, the major theme of art in all its aspects, the principal industry of Hollywood and of countless magazines, the thing with which human beings are most concerned all their lives, the most important experience in the world, *love* is something about which most of us, at this late date, are still extremely vague. One has only to ask one's friends what they understand by "love" to discover how unclear the idea remains in the minds of many people. Even when a fair definition is achieved the meaning of love in its full significance is rarely understood.

In this chapter I should like to set out some of the findings about the nature and meaning of love as scientists have revealed them.

The dictionary tells us that love is a feeling of deep regard, fondness, and devotion. Robert Louis Stevenson said that love was a passionate kindness. One could go on quoting hundreds of statements about love, and they would all be true as far as they go, but none of them go far

"A Scientist Looks at Love" by Ashley Montagu. From *The Humanization of Man* (New York: World Publishing Company, 1962), pp. 99–112. Reprinted by permission of the author.

enough because while they provide the skeleton, they miss the vital essence of the meaning of love. This essential meaning one can discover only by studying the origins and development of love as they are manifested in small children, in the newborn baby and every stage of childhood, and finally in adolescents and in adults.

There is a widespread belief that a newborn baby is a rather selfish, disorganized, or unorganized, wild kind of creature which would grow into a violently intractable savage if it were not properly disciplined. Contrary to this widely held belief, modern scientists find that far from being such an unorganized barbarian the newborn baby is one of the most highly organized creatures on the face of the earth, and organized not for brattishness but for love.

The newborn baby is organized in an extraordinarily sensitive manner, most delicately attuned to receive all those stimulations which will creatively contribute to its development. Far from wanting to be disciplined in the usual meaning of that word, it wants to be loved. It behaves as if it expected to be loved, and when its expectation is thwarted—that is, frustrated—it behaves in a grievously disappointed manner.

There is now good evidence which leads us to believe that not only does a baby want to be loved, but also that it wants to love, that all its drives are oriented in the direction of receiving and giving love, and that if it doesn't receive love it is unable to give it—as a child or as an adult.

From the moment of birth the baby needs the reciprocal exchange of love with its mother. From the very outset the baby is capable of conferring great benefits upon the mother—*if* the maternal-infant relationship is not disturbed. It has now been thoroughly established that if the baby is left with the mother and put to nurse at her breast, three problems which have bedeviled obstetricians for many years, and what is more important, have been responsible for much tragedy and unhappiness, are in most cases solved at once. These are hemorrhaging from the womb after birth, the beginning return of the uterus to normal size, and the completion of the third stage of labor by the ejection of the placenta. These problems are solved in the majority of instances by putting the baby to nurse at the mother's breast. The hemorrhage is reduced and the uterus begins its return to almost normal size within a matter of minutes, and the placenta becomes detached and is ejected. There are almost certainly other benefits which the nursing baby confers upon the mother, not the least of which are probably psychological. The baby is in turn, of course, also benefited; among other things, such a baby is practically never a feeding problem.

Understanding just these things helps us to understand better, or begin to understand, the meaning of love, *if* the nursing maternal-infant relationship and its effects in any way involve the elements of love. It has, I believe, universally been acknowledged that the mother-infant relationship perhaps more than any other defines the very essence of love. If that is so, then on the basis of the findings I have already described we may tentatively define love as *the relationship between persons in which they confer mutual benefits upon each other.* This is a broad definition and might be said well to describe the relationship which exists between an insurance company and the insured. Bearing in mind the physiological benefits which accrue to mother and child, perhaps we could try again and say that *love is the relationship between persons which contributes to the welfare and development of each.*

The "welfare" given the mother in the cited example consisted of reduced hemorrhage, the initiation of the reduction to normal size of the maternal uterus, and the completion of the third stage of labor. In the baby there are established good feeding habits, and there is a healthy development of the gastrointestinal, genito-urinary, and respiratory tracts—indeed, of all the sustaining systems of the body. Scientists have learned most about love from the study of the mother-infant relationships. Let us proceed to the discussion of *how* and *what* they have learned about the nature and meaning of love.

Survival is of the first importance, without it nothing else matters, but survival alone is not enough—human beings need and should receive much more. If children are to grow in health and harmony, then they must experience more than the mere physical satisfaction of their needs. A baby is a beginning human being, and his birthright is development—development of his psychological and spiritual as well as his physical potentialities for being human. The mere satisfaction of his physical needs will not bring about such development—such satisfaction may secure survival, but in most cases it is doubtful whether it will even secure that.

We now know that babies who are physically well nurtured may nevertheless waste away and die unless they are also loved. We also know that the only thing that can rescue such babies when they are dying is love. We now know, beyond cavil or question, that love is an essential part of the nourishment of every baby, and that unless human beings in their early stages of development are loved they will not grow and develop as healthy organisms. It has taken the independent observations of a number of physicians and other investigators to ascertain the relationship between the infant's need for love and his capacity to survive.

It may come as a surprise to many readers to learn that because this relationship was not understood during the first two decades of this century, the majority of infants under one year of age who entered hospitals and similar institutions never emerged from them alive. This shocking infant death rate was discussed at a meeting of the American Pediatric Society in 1915. Dr. Henry Chapin reported on ten infant asylums located in the United States in which, with one exception, *every* infant under two years of age died! Dr. R. Hamil of Philadelphia, at the same meeting, remarked with somber irony that he "had the honor to be connected with an institution in Philadelphia in which the mortality among all the infants under one year of age, when admitted to the institution and retained there for any length of time, was 100 per cent. That is, no infant admitted under one year of age lived to be two years old." Dr. T. S. Southworth of New York City, said, "I can give an instance from an institution which no longer exists in which on account of the very considerable mortality among the infants admitted, it was customary to enter the condition of every infant on the admission card as hopeless. That covered all subsequent happenings." [1]

Many other such reports could be quoted from other American authorities as well as from institutions abroad, but those given above should be enough. In the late twenties Dr. J. Brennemann of New York City recognized the ill effects caused by an absence of mothering and established a rule in his hospital that every baby should be picked up, carried about, amused, and "mothered" several times a day.[2] A most illuminating experience is related by Dr. Fritz Talbot, who visited the Children's Clinic in Düsseldorf, Germany, shortly before the First World War. Dr. Talbot noticed a fat old woman waddling down a corridor with a baby on her hip. Querying the chief of the Clinic, he was told, "Oh, that's Old Anna. Whenever we have a baby for whom everything we could do has failed, we turn it over to Old Anna. She is always successful." [3]

Drs. Ruth and Harry Bakwin, of Bellevue Hospital Pediatric Division, have graphically described what happens in hospitals as a result of the lacklove experiences which children undergo there:

---

[1] H. D. Chapin, "A Plea for Accurate Statistics in Infants' Institutions," *Transactions of the American Pediatric Society*, 27 (1915), 180 ff.

[2] J. Brennemann, "The Infant Ward," *American Journal of Diseases of Children*, 43 (1932), 577.

[3] *Ibid.*

The effect of residence in a hospital manifests itself by a fairly well-defined clinical picture. A striking feature is the failure to gain properly, despite the ingestion of diets which are entirely adequate for growth in the home. Infants in hospitals sleep less than others and they rarely smile or babble spontaneously. They are listless and apathetic and look unhappy. The appetite is indifferent and food is accepted without enthusiasm. The stools tend to be frequent and, in sharp contrast with infants cared for in the home, it is unusual for 24 hours to pass without an evacuation. Respiratory infections which last only a day or two in the home are prolonged and may persist for weeks or months. Return to the home results in defervescence (disappearance of fever) within a few days and a prompt and striking gain in weight.[4]

The emotional deprivation suffered by infants in hospitals may do vastly more damage than the physical condition which brought them there. The infant can suffer no greater loss than the privation of its mother's love. There is an old Talmudic proverb which has it that since God could not be everywhere he created mothers. There have been several important studies of the effects of the absence of mother-love within the past decade.

Dr. René Spitz of New York City has reported on children confined in two different institutions. They were studied simultaneously during the first year of life. Both institutions were adequate in all physical respects, providing equivalent housing, asepsis, food, and hygiene. In both, infants were admitted shortly after birth. The institutions differed in but one factor—the amount of affection offered. In the first institution, called "Nursery," the infants were cared for by their own mothers. In the second institution, called "Foundlinghome," the children were raised from the third month by overworked nursing personnel, each nurse in charge of from eight to twelve children. The absence or presence of emotional interchange between mother and child formed the one independent condition in the comparison of the two groups.

The response to this condition showed up in many ways, but perhaps most comprehensively in what is called the Developmental Quotient. The Developmental Quotient represents a measure of the total development of six sectors of the personality: mastery of perception, bodily functions, social relations, memory and imitation, manipulative ability, and intelligence. At the end of the first year, though the "Foundlinghome" infants had a developmental quotient of 124 to start with, and the "Nursery" infants a developmental quotient of 101.5, the

[4] Ruth M. and Harry Bakwin, *Psychologic Care during Infancy and Childhood* (New York, Appleton-Century, 1942), p. 295.

deprived "Foundlinghome" infants declined to a developmental quotient of 72, while the "Nursery" infants rose to 105. At the end of the second year the D.Q. had fallen in the "Foundlinghome" group to an astonishing low of 45!

As Dr. Spitz remarks:

> We have here an impressive example of how the absence of one psychosocial factor, that of emotional interchange with the mother, results in a complete reversal of a developmental trend.
>
> It should be realized that the factor which was present in the first case but eliminated in the second, is the pivot of all development in the first year. It is the mother-child relation. By choosing this factor as our independent variable we were able to observe its vital importance. While the children in "Nursery" developed into normal healthy toddlers, a two-year observation of "Foundlinghome" showed that the emotionally starved children never learned to speak, to walk, to feed themselves. With one or two exceptions in a total of 91 children, those who survived were human wrecks who behaved either in the manner of agitated or apathetic idiots.[5]

A comparison of the mortality rates in the two institutions is striking and significant. During five years of observation involving 239 children who had been institutionalized for one year or more, "Nursery" did not lose a single child through death; whereas in "Foundlinghome" 37 per cent of the children died during a two years' observation period. Death, Dr. Spitz states, is but an extreme consequence of the general physiological and psychological decline which affects children completely starved of emotional interchange.

Drs. Ralph Fried and M. F. Mayer of Cleveland, in a study[6] of dependent and neglected children at the Cleveland Jewish Orphans Home, found the severest disturbances in growth and development to be in these emotionally impoverished derelict children. The child that has been inadequately loved, neglected, or abandoned by its parents, exhibits socio-emotional disturbances which are reflected in his growth and development. Drs. Fried and Mayer conclude that "socio-emotional adjustment plays not merely an important but actually a crucial role among all the factors that determine individual health and physical well-being . . . it has become clear that socio-emotional disturbances tend to affect physical growth adversely, and that growth

[5] René Spitz, "Anaclitic Depression," *The Psychoanalytic Study of the Child*, vol. 2 (New York, International Universities Press, 1947), pp. 313–342.

[6] Ralph Fried and M. F. Mayer, "Socio-Emotional Factors Accounting for Growth Failure of Children Living in an Institution," *Journal of Pediatrics*, 33 (1948), 444–56.

failure so caused is much more frequent and more extensive than is generally recognized."

Dr. Griffith Binning, in a study[7] of 800 Canadian (Saskatoon) children, found "that events in the child's life that caused separation from one or both parents—death, divorce, enlistment of a parent—and a mental environment which gave the child a feeling that normal love and affection was lacking did far more damage to growth than did disease," indeed, that such an environment "was more serious than all other factors combined." Dr. Binning was able to show that where disease has affected growth "in most cases the reason is the emotional tension arising from the disease and its manner of treatment rather than the disease itself."

Drs. N. B. Talbot, E. H. Sobel, B. S. Burke, E. Lindemann, and S. S. Kaufman, of Massachusetts General Hospital, Boston, in a study[8] of fifty-one children who exhibited stunted growth, but in whom no physical abnormalities could be found to account for their dwarfism, found that "the majority were undernourished because of anorexia [chronic lack of appetite] due to either emotional disturbances or mental deficiency or a combination of both, in addition to such factors as parental poverty and ignorance. In the fifty-one so studied there was a high incidence of rejection by the mother, emotional disturbances and delinquency in mothers, marked poverty at home. Fourteen per cent had severe emotional reactions with chronic grief and anorexia attributable to broken homes brought about by death, divorce and desertion."

Drs. H. Lihn, Karl Menninger, and M. Mayman of the Menninger Clinic, Topeka, Kansas, have found that in the infant and childhood histories of adult chronic osteoarthritic patients, there was, without exception, the experience, in varying degrees, of being ignored, neglected, or rejected by their overburdened or inconsiderate parents. Often these patients were the victims of early desertion and of the arid emotional conditions of the orphanage.[9]

There exists much additional research along the same lines,[10] but that given above should be sufficient to indicate that emotional

---

[7] Griffith Binning, "Peace Be on Thy House," *Health* (March/April, 1948), pp. 6–7, 28, 30.

[8] N. B. Talbot et al., "Dwarfism in Healthy Children: Its Possible Relation to Emotional Disturbances," *New England Journal of Medicine*, 236 (1947), 783–93.

[9] H. Lihn et al., "Personality Factors in Osteo-arthritis," in *Life Stress and Bodily Disease*, H. G. Wolff et al., eds. (Baltimore, Williams & Wilkins, 1950), pp. 744–49.

[10] For a review of that research see Ashley Montagu, *The Direction of Human Development*, Rev. ed. (New York, Hawthorn Books, 1970). See also Ashley Montagu, ed., *Culture and Human Development* (Englewood Cliffs, N.J., Prentice-Hall, Inc., 1974).

deprivation during childhood may result in severe retardations in growth and development of the total organism. The effects upon the development of personality and behavior of a lacklove infancy appear to be even more severe.

Criminal, delinquent, neurotic, psychopathic, asocial, and similar forms of unfortunate behavior can, in the majority of cases, be traced to a childhood history of inadequate love and emotional instability. Findings on this score have been surveyed in a United Nations World Health Organization report entitled *Maternal Care and Mental Health*. Dr. John Bowlby, the English psychiatrist who prepared the survey, had published one of the earliest studies on the relationship between maternal love and juvenile delinquency.

In a study[11] of forty-four juvenile thieves Dr. Bowlby found that a large proportion exhibited an inability to establish affectionate relationships with other persons, and displayed what he termed "the affectionless character." Fourteen of the forty-four delinquents were of this type, and of these fourteen, twelve had suffered a prolonged separation from the mother at an early age. These affectionless characters were significantly more delinquent than the other thieves, "constituting more than half of the more serious and chronic offenders."

Drs. Fritz Redl and David Wineman of Detroit have much the same story to tell in their book *Children Who Hate* (Glencoe, Ill., Free Press, 1951), as does Dr. Frank Cohen of New York in his book *Children in Trouble* (New York, Norton, 1952).

Show me a murderer, a hardened criminal, a juvenile delinquent, a psychopath, and a "cold fish," and in almost every case I will show you the tragedy that results from not being adequately loved during childhood. When the infant's expectation of emotional warmth and love is thwarted, he may turn in upon himself for any satisfactions he can secure. If his crying goes unnoticed he may begin to weep through his skin, and break out in many kinds of skin disturbances; or he may begin to weep and wheeze through his lungs in the form of asthma, or he may break out in ulcers of the gastrointestinal tract—yes, in infancy, not only in adulthood. In short, in order to attract the attention he so much desires and needs, he will resort to every conceivable means at his disposal. On the psychological level this will usually take the form of behavior calculated to elicit the required attention. We generally call such behavior "aggressive." But when it is

[11] John Bowlby, "Forty-Four Juvenile Thieves: Their Characters and Home Life," *International Journal of Psychoanalysis*, 25 (1944), 19–53, 122, 154–78.

fully understood we find that aggressive behavior is, frequently, nothing but love frustrated, a technique for compelling love. Hence, it should be very clear that the best possible way in which to approach aggressive behavior in children is not by further aggressive behavior toward them, but with love. And this is true not only for children but for human beings at all other ages.

Why do criminals so often enjoy having their photographs in the papers? Is it not perhaps for the same reason that they have committed their crimes? Is it not because these were the only ways they knew how to gain the attention they had been denied, and at the same time to revenge themselves upon the society which had let them down, disillusioned, deserted, and dehumanized them?

Why do rejected children often steal from their mothers? Dr. Adrian Vander Veer offers an explanation:[12] "The stealing usually has very little to do with money . . . the stealing really means that the child is trying to get something, in a vague way, that he knows he hasn't got, which something is his mother's love. If this delinquent pattern becomes marked enough, it may form the foundation for later more generalized anti-social behavior, all sorts of crimes, for example, stealing from persons who are not in the family." Dr. Vander Veer is more emphatic. He says that maternal rejection may be seen as the "causative factor in almost every type and every individual case of neurosis or behavior problem in children."

The mother does not necessarily have to be the biological mother of the child; any human being whether female or male, as long as he is capable of giving the child love, may be the equivalent of the real mother. All investigators are agreed that the importance of the mother—biological or surrogate—lies in the fact that she is the first representative of humanity with whom the child comes into association and through whom it usually receives the satisfaction or expects to receive the satisfaction of its needs. The child constructs its picture of the world largely through the experience it has with its mother. According as the mother is loving or unloving, the child will feel that the world is loving or unloving.

Endowed at birth with all the necessary drives for developing as a loving harmonic human being, the child learns to love by being loved. When it is not loved it fails to learn to love, but responds instead with protesting behavior, with rage and aggression, then with despair, and

[12] A. Vander Veer, *The Unwanted Child*, Publication of the Illinois League For Planned Parenthood, Chicago, April 10, 1949, pp. 3-12.

finally with the abandonment of all faith and hope in human beings. These are not mere statements concocted out of a desk thinker's head, but the conclusions of the workers at The International Children's Centre in Paris under the leadership of Drs. John Bowlby and Jenny Roudinesco. Such children, the children who have not been adequately loved, grow up to be persons who find it extremely difficult to understand the meaning of love; they are awkward in their human relationships, "cold fish," they tend to be thoughtless and inconsiderate; they have little emotional depth; hence they are able to enter into all sorts of human relationships in a shallow way and drift from one marriage to another with the greatest emotional ease. They are "affectionless characters" who suffer from a hunger for affection. Awkward and ineffectual in their attempts to secure it, they often suffer rejection and end up by becoming more embittered than ever, finding themselves in the paradoxical situation of hating people because they want to love them, but having attempted to love them have been repulsed, and so end up by hating them. One such affectionless character who was apprehended by the police for having killed an entire family of five strangers exclaimed, "The whole world hates my guts, and I hate the whole world's guts." This youth had never been loved by anyone; whenever he made the attempt he was misunderstood and rejected. He served several prison terms and was so full of hate that his next crime could easily have been predicted . . . and prevented. Our society, murderously logical, corrected the wrongs thus done by murdering the murderer.

Many such unloved children avoid coming into overt conflict with society by making the required external adjustments, but they still remain cold, desolate, and hungry for love. Such children as adults often seek ways of achieving power, as if by so doing they may be able to force others to love them. Unhappily for them and for many others whom they may involve in their schemes, they rarely succeed. Such persons wreak much havoc upon their fellow human beings when, as in the case of such unloved creatures as Adolf Hitler, Mussolini, and Stalin, they attain positions of great worldly power. It was quite evident that the tragedy these men brought to the world was principally due to the incapacity of these creatures to love or to understand the meaning of love. Had they understood the meaning of love, had they been taught how to love by having been loved themselves, they could not possibly have behaved as inhumanly as they did. To love your neighbor as yourself requires first that you be able to love yourself, and the only way one learns that art is by having been adequately loved during the first six years of one's life. As Freud pointed out, this is the period during which the foundations of the personality are either well and truly laid—or not. If one doesn't love oneself one cannot love others. To make loving order in the world we must first have had loving order made in ourselves.

We are now, perhaps, in a better position to understand the meaning and importance of love for human beings and for humanity. Nothing in the world can be more important or as significant. Let us, then, set out the characteristics as best we can, of love—the conditions which must be fulfilled if we are to agree that the state of love exists.

- Love is not only a subjective feeling which one has, an emotion, but a series of acts by means of which one conveys to another the feeling that someone is deeply involved, profoundly interested, in him and in his welfare. In this sense love is demonstrative, it is sacrificial, it is self-abnegative. It always puts the other first. It is not a cold or calculated altruism, but a feeling of deep involvement in the other.

- Love is unconditional—it makes no bargains, it trades with no one for anything, but conveys the feeling, the in-the-bones belief to the other that you are all for him, that you are there to give him your support, to contribute to his development as best you can, because the other is what he is, *not* because he is something you want or expect him to be, but because you value him for what he is as he is.

- Love is supportive—it conveys to the other that you will never commit that supreme of all the treasons that one human being can commit against another, namely, to let him down when he most needs you. Love promises that you will always be present to support the other, no matter what the conditions you will never fail him; that you will neither condemn nor condone, but that you will always be there to offer your sympathy and your understanding, and that whatever the other needs as a human being he shall have, even though it may be a firm no. Love means that you will be there to help him say yes to life, and to have all his needs for love satisfied.

If a human being can convey this complex of feelings to another, then the state of love for that other can be said to exist.

From the evidence thus far available it seems clear that love is indispensably necessary for the healthy development of the individual. Love is the principal developer of one's capacity for being human—it is the chief stimulus to the development of social competence, and the only thing in the world that can produce that sense of belongingness and relatedness to the world of humanity which every mentally healthy human being develops. And what is mental health? Mental health is the ability to love, the ability to work, and the ability to play.

And what is love? Love is the quality which confers survival benefits upon others, and upon oneself, in a creatively enlarging manner.

Love is creative—creative both for the receiver and the giver, and greatly enriching the lives of both. When we understand the meaning of love we understand that it is the only thing in the world of which one cannot give anyone too much. The counterfeit thing is not the real thing—overprotectiveness and "smothering" are often mistaken for love when they are in fact often disguises for hostility. Genuine love can never harm or inhibit, it can only benefit and create freedom and order. Love has a firmness and discipline of its own for which there can be no substitute. No child can ever be spoiled by love, and there are few if any human problems that cannot be most efficiently solved by its application.

Scientists are discovering at this very moment that to live as if to live and love were one is the only way of life for human beings, because, indeed, this is the way of life which the innate nature of man demands. We are discovering that the highest ideals of man spring from man's own nature, that what is right for man is what is right for his nature, and that the highest of these innately based ideals is the one that must enliven and inform all his other ideals, namely, *love.* This is not a new discovery in the world; what is new is that scientists should be rediscovering these truths by scientific means. Contemporary scientists working in this field are giving a scientific foundation or validation to the Sermon on the Mount, to the Golden Rule: To do unto others as you would have them do unto you, and to love your neighbor as yourself.

We have left the study of love to the last, but now that we can begin to understand its importance for humanity, we can see that here is the area in which the men of religion, the educators, the physicians, and the scientists can join hands in the common endeavor of putting man back upon the road of his evolutionary destiny from which he has wandered so far away—the road that leads to health and happiness for all humanity, and that oft-invoked peace and good will unto all on earth.

HARRY F. HARLOW

The Nature of Love*

In this contribution Professor Harlow gives an illuminating account of his famous experiments on the nature of love. His opening comments draw attention to "the apparent repression of love by modern psychologists," and he might have added, also by other scientists. As for politicians, it is a matter of record that when Professor Harlow received a grant from a government sponsoring body, the matter was raised in the U.S. Senate, where the idea of money being spent for research on such a subject as love was greeted with laughter and derision. The grant was a substantial one, but not nearly as substantial as the results returned by Professor Harlow, whose work represents the pioneering, fundamental, and classical scientific study of man's most important behavior.

One of the major demonstrations of Harlow's experiments has been the proof of the importance of body contact in the development of affectionate behavior. This is an awareness which in the modern world has been largely lost; seldom has it been the subject of scientific study.[1] The importance of satisfying the infant's needs for bodily contact, for being held and cuddled, are underscored as a result of Harlow's findings, carrying messages to a dehumanizing world of which that world stands greatly in need.

Love is a wondrous state, deep, tender, and rewarding. Because of its intimate and personal nature it is regarded by some as an improper topic for experimental research. But, whatever our personal feelings may be, our assigned mission as psychologists is to analyze all facets of

"The Nature of Love" by Harry F. Harlow. From *The American Psychologist*, Vol. 13, No. 12, December 1958, pp. 673–85. Copyright © 1958 by the American Psychological Association. Reprinted by permission. All illustrations and charts have been omitted.

---

* Address of the President at the sixty-sixth Annual Convention of the American Psychological Association, Washington, D.C., August 31, 1958.

The researches reported in this paper were supported by funds supplied by Grant No. M-722, National Institutes of Health, by a grant from the Ford Foundation, and by funds received from the Graduate School of the University of Wisconsin.

[1] See Ashley Montagu, *Touching: The Human Significance of the Skin* (New York: Columbia University Press, 1971); Harper & Row Perennial Books, 1972).

human and animal behavior into their component variables. So far as love or affection is concerned, psychologists have failed in this mission. The little we know about love does not transcend simple observation, and the little we write about it has been written better by poets and novelists. But of greater concern is the fact that psychologists tend to give progressively less attention to a motive which pervades our entire lives. Psychologists, at least psychologists who write textbooks, not only show no interest in the origin and development of love or affection, but they seem to be unaware of its very existence.

The apparent repression of love by modern psychologists stands in sharp contrast with the attitude taken by many famous and normal people. The word "love" has the highest reference frequency of any word cited in Bartlett's book of *Familiar Quotations*. It would appear that this emotion has long had a vast interest and fascination for human beings, regardless of the attitude taken by psychologists; but the quotations cited, even by famous and normal people, have a mundane redundancy. These authors and authorities have stolen love from the child and infant and made it the exclusive property of the adolescent and adult.

Thoughtful men, and probably all women, have speculated on the nature of love. From the developmental point of view, the general plan is quite clear: The initial love responses of the human being are those made by the infant to the mother or some mother surrogate. From this intimate attachment of the child to the mother, multiple learned and generalized affectional responses are formed.

Unfortunately, beyond these simple facts we know little about the fundamental variables underlying the formation of affectional responses and little about the mechanisms through which the love of the infant for the mother develops into the multifaceted response patterns characterizing love or affection in the adult. Because of the dearth of experimentation, theories about the fundamental nature of affection have evolved at the level of observation, intuition, and discerning guesswork, whether these have been proposed by psychologists, sociologists, anthropologists, physicians, or psychoanalysts.

The position commonly held by psychologists and sociologists is quite clear: The basic motives are, for the most part, the primary drives—particularly hunger, thirst, elimination, pain, and sex—and all other motives, including love or affection, are derived or secondary drives. The mother is associated with the reduction of the primary drives—particularly hunger, thirst, and pain—and through learning, affection or love is derived.

It is entirely reasonable to believe that the mother through association with food may become a secondary-reinforcing agent, but this is an inadequate mechanism to account for the persistence of the infant-maternal ties. There is a spate of researches on the formation of secondary reinforcers to hunger and thirst reduction. There can be no question that almost any external stimulus can become a secondary reinforcer if properly associated with tissue-need reduction, but the fact remains that this redundant literature demonstrates unequivocally that such derived drives suffer relatively rapid experimental extinction. Contrariwise, human affection does not extinguish when the mother ceases to have intimate association with the drives in question. Instead, the affectional ties to the mother show a lifelong, unrelenting persistence and, even more surprising, widely expanding generality.

Oddly enough, one of the few psychologists who took a position counter to modern psychological dogma was John B. Watson, who believed that love was an innate emotion elicited by cutaneous stimulation of the erogenous zones. But experimental psychologists, with their peculiar propensity to discover facts that are not true, brushed this theory aside by demonstrating that the human neonate had no differentiable emotions, and they established a fundamental psychological law that prophets are without honor in their own profession.

The psychoanalysts have concerned themselves with the problem of the nature of the development of love in the neonate and infant, using ill and aging human beings as subjects. They have discovered the overwhelming importance of the breast and related this to the oral erotic tendencies developed at an age preceding their subjects' memories. Their theories range from a belief that the infant has an innate need to achieve and suckle at the breast to beliefs not unlike commonly accepted psychological theories. There are exceptions, as seen in the recent writings of John Bowlby, who attributes importance not only to food and thirst satisfaction, but also to "primary object-clinging," a need for intimate physical contact, which is initially associated with the mother.

As far as I know, there exists no direct experimental analysis of the relative importance of the stimulus variables determining the affectional or love responses in the neonatal and infant primate. Unfortunately, the human neonate is a limited experimental subject for such researches because of his inadequate motor capabilities. By the time the human infant's motor responses can be precisely measured, the antecedent determining conditions cannot be defined, having been lost in a jumble and jungle of confounded variables.

Many of these difficulties can be resolved by the use of the neonatal and infant macaque monkey as the subject for the analysis of basic affectional variables. It is possible to make precise measurements in this primate beginning at two to ten days of age, depending upon the maturational status of the individual animal at birth. The macaque infant differs from the human infant in that the monkey is more mature at birth and grows more rapidly; but the basic responses relating to affection, including nursing, contact, clinging, and even visual and auditory exploration, exhibit no fundamental differences in the two species. Even the development of perception, fear, frustration, and learning capability follows very similar sequences in rhesus monkeys and human children.

Three years' experimentation before we started our studies on affection gave us experience with the neonatal monkey. We had separated more than 60 of these animals from their mothers 6 to 12 hours after birth and suckled them on tiny bottles. The infant mortality was only a small fraction of what would have obtained had we let the monkey mothers raise their infants. Our bottle-fed babies were healthier and heavier than monkey-mother-reared infants. We know that we are better monkey mothers than are real monkey mothers thanks to synthetic diets, vitamins, iron extracts, penicillin, chloromycetin, 5% glucose, and constant, tender, loving care.

During the course of these studies we noticed that the laboratory-raised babies showed strong attachment to the cloth pads (folded gauze diapers) which were used to cover the hardware-cloth floors of their cages. The infants clung to these pads and engaged in violent temper tantrums when the pads were removed and replaced for sanitary reasons. Such contact-need or responsiveness had been reported previously by Gertrude van Wagenen for the monkey and by Thomas McCulloch and George Haslerud for the chimpanzee and is reminiscent of the devotion often exhibited by human infants to their pillows, blankets, and soft, cuddly stuffed toys. The baby, human or monkey, if it is to survive, must clutch at more than a straw.

We had also discovered during some allied observational studies that a baby monkey raised on a bare wire-mesh cage floor survives with difficulty, if at all, during the first five days of life. If a wire-mesh cone is introduced, the baby does better; and, if the cone is covered with terry cloth, husky, healthy, happy babies evolve. It takes more than a baby and a box to make a normal monkey. We were impressed by the possibility that, above and beyond the bubbling fountain of breast or bottle, contact comfort might be a very important variable in the development of the infant's affection for the mother.

At this point we decided to study the development of affectional responses of neonatal and infant monkeys to an artificial, inanimate mother, and so we built a surrogate mother which we hoped and believed would be a good surrogate mother. In devising this surrogate mother we were dependent neither upon the capriciousness of evolutionary processes nor upon mutations produced by chance radioactive fallout. Instead, we designed the mother surrogate in terms of modern human-engineering principles. We produced a perfectly proportioned, streamlined body stripped of unnecessary bulges and appendices. Redundancy in the surrogate mother's system was avoided by reducing the number of breasts from two to one and placing this unibreast in an upper-thoracic, sagittal position, thus maximizing the natural and known perceptual-motor capabilities of the infant operator. The surrogate was made from a block of wood, covered with sponge rubber, and sheathed in tan cotton terry cloth. A light bulb behind her radiated heat. The result was a mother, soft, warm, and tender, a mother with infinite patience, a mother available twenty-four hours a day, a mother that never scolded her infant and never struck or bit her baby in anger. Furthermore, we designed a mother-machine with maximal maintenance efficiency since failure of any system or function could be resolved by the simple substitution of black boxes and new component parts. It is our opinion that we engineered a very superior monkey mother, although this position is not held universally by the monkey fathers.

Before beginning our initial experiment we also designed and constructed a second mother surrogate, a surrogate in which we deliberately built less than the maximal capability for contact comfort. She is made of wire-mesh, a substance entirely adequate to provide postural support and nursing capability, and she is warmed by radiant heat. Her body differs in no essential way from that of the cloth mother surrogate other than in the quality of the contact comfort which she can supply.

In our initial experiment, the dual mother-surrogate condition, a cloth mother and a wire mother were placed in different cubicles attached to the infant's living cage. For four newborn monkeys the cloth mother lactated and the wire mother did not; and, for the other four, this condition was reversed. In either condition the infant received all its milk through the mother surrogate as soon as it was able to maintain itself in this way, a capability achieved within two or three days except in the case of very immature infants. Supplementary feedings were given until the milk intake from the mother surrogate was adequate. Thus, the experiment was designed as a test of the relative importance of the variables of contact comfort and nursing comfort. During the first 14 days of life the monkey's cage floor was covered with a heating pad wrapped in a folded gauze diaper, and thereafter the cage floor was bare. The infants were always free to leave the heating pad or cage floor to contact either mother, and the time spent on the surrogate mothers was automatically recorded. The data make it obvious that contact comfort is a variable of overwhelming importance in the development of affectional responses, whereas lactation is a variable of negligible importance. With age and opportunity to learn, subjects with the lactating wire mother showed decreasing responsiveness to her and increasing responsiveness to the nonlactating cloth mother, a finding completely contrary to any interpretation of derived drive in which the mother-form becomes conditioned to hunger-thirst reduction. These differential responses persisted throughout 165 consecutive days of testing.

One control group of neonatal monkeys was raised on a single wire mother, and a second control group was raised on a single cloth mother. There were no differences between these two groups in amount of milk ingested or in weight gain. The only difference between the groups lay in the composition of the feces, the softer stools of the wire-mother infants suggesting psychosomatic involvement. The wire mother is biologically adequate but psychologically inept.

We were not surprised to discover that contact comfort was an important basic affectional or love variable, but we did not expect it to overshadow so completely the variable of nursing; indeed, the disparity is so great as to suggest that the primary function of nursing as an affectional variable is that of insuring frequent and intimate body contact of the infant with the mother. Certainly, man cannot live by milk alone. Love is an emotion that does not need to be bottle- or spoon-fed, and we may be sure that there is nothing to be gained by giving lip service to love.

A charming lady once heard me describe these experiments; and, when I subsequently talked to her, her face brightened with sudden insight: "Now I know what's wrong with me," she said, "I'm just a wire mother." Perhaps she was lucky. She might have been a wire wife.

We believe that contact comfort has long served the animal kingdom as a motivating agent for affectional responses. Since at the present time we have no experimental data to substantiate this position, we supply information which must be accepted, if at all, on the basis of face validity.

One function of the real mother, human or subhuman and presumably of a mother surrogate is to provide a haven of safety for the infant in times of fear and danger. The frightened or ailing child clings to its mother, not its father; and this selective responsiveness in times of distress, disturbance, or danger may be used as a measure of the strength of affectional bonds. We have tested this kind of differential responsiveness by presenting to the infants in their cages, in the presence of the two mothers, various fear-producing stimuli such as a moving toy bear. It is apparent that the cloth mother is highly preferred over the wire one, and this differential selectivity is enhanced by age and experience. In this situation, the variable of nursing appears to be of absolutely no importance: the infant consistently seeks the soft mother surrogate regardless of nursing condition.

Similarly, the mother or mother surrogate provides its young with a source of security, and this role or function is seen with special clarity when mother and child are in a strange situation. At the present time we have completed tests for this relationship on four of our eight baby monkeys assigned to the dual mother-surrogate condition by introducing them for three minutes into the strange environment of a room measuring six feet by six feet by six feet (also called the "open-field test") and containing multiple stimuli known to elicit curiosity-manipulatory responses in baby monkeys. The subjects were placed in this situation twice a week for eight weeks with no mother surrogate present during alternate sessions and the cloth mother present during the others. A cloth diaper was always available as one of the stimuli throughout all sessions. After one or two adaptation sessions, the infants always rushed to the mother surrogate when she was present and clutched her, rubbed their bodies against her, and frequently manipulated her body and face. After a few additional sessions, the infants began to use the mother surrogate as a source of security, a base of operations. They would explore and manipulate a stimulus and then return to the mother before adventuring again into the strange new world. The behavior of these infants was quite different when the mother was absent from the room. Frequently they would freeze in a crouched position. Emotionality indices such as vocalization, crouching, rocking, and sucking increased sharply. Total emotionality score was cut in half when the mother was present. In the absence of the mother some of the experimental monkeys would rush to the center of the room where the mother was customarily placed and then run rapidly from object to object, screaming and crying all the while. Continuous, frantic clutching of their bodies was very common, even when not in the crouching position. These monkeys frequently contacted and clutched the cloth diaper, but this action never pacified them. The same behavior occurred in the presence of the wire mother. No difference between the cloth-mother-fed and wire-mother-fed infants was demonstrated under either condition. Four control infants never raised with a mother surrogate showed the same emotionality scores when the mother was absent as the experimental infants showed in the absence of the mother, but the controls' scores were slightly larger in the presence of the mother surrogate than in her absence.

Some years ago Robert Butler demonstrated that mature monkeys enclosed in a dimly lighted box would open and reopen a door hour after hour for no other reward than that of looking outside the box. We now have data indicating that neonatal monkeys show this same compulsive visual curiosity on their first test day in an adaptation of the Butler apparatus which we call the "love machine," an apparatus designed to measure love. Usually these tests are begun when the monkey is 10 days of age, but this same persistent visual exploration has been obtained in a three-day-old monkey during the first half-hour of testing. Butler also demonstrated that rhesus monkeys show selectivity in rate and frequency of door-opening to stimuli of differential attractiveness in the visual field outside the box. We have utilized this principle of response selectivity by the monkey to measure strength of affectional responsiveness in our infants in the baby version of the Butler box. The test sequence involves four repetitions of a test battery in which four stimuli—cloth mother, wire mother, infant monkey, and empty box—are presented for a 30-minute period on successive days. The first four subjects in the dual mother-surrogate group were given a single test sequence at 40 to 50 days of age, depending upon the availability of the apparatus, and only their data are presented. The second set of four subjects is being given repetitive tests to obtain information relating to the development of visual exploration. The data obtained from the first four infants raised with the two mother surrogates show approximately equal responding to the cloth mother and another infant monkey, and no greater responsiveness to the wire mother than to an empty box. Again, the results are independent of the kind of mother that lactated, cloth or wire. The same results are found for a control group raised, but not fed, on a single cloth mother. Contrariwise, no differential responsiveness [was shown] to cloth and wire mothers by a second control group, which was not raised on any mother surrogate. We can be certain that not all love is blind.

The first four infant monkeys in the dual mother-surrogate group were separated from their mothers between 165 and 170 days of age and tested for retention during the following 9 days and then at 30-day intervals for six successive months. In keeping with the data obtained on adult monkeys by Butler, we find a high rate of responding to any stimulus, even the empty box. But throughout the entire 185-day retention period there is a consistent and significant difference in response frequency to the cloth mother contrasted with either the wire mother or the empty box, and no consistent difference between wire mother and empty box.

Affectional retention was also tested in the open field during the first 9 days after separation and then at 30-day intervals, and each test condition was run twice at each retention interval. The infant's behavior differed from that observed during the period preceding separation. When the cloth mother was present in the post-separation period, the babies rushed to her, climbed up, clung tightly to her, and rubbed their heads and faces against her body. After this initial embrace and reunion, they played on the mother, including biting and tearing at her cloth cover; but they rarely made any attempt to leave her during the test period, nor did they manipulate or play with the objects in the room, in contrast with their behavior before maternal separation. The only exception was the occasional monkey that left the mother surrogate momentarily, grasped the folded piece of paper (one of the standard stimuli in the field), and brought it quickly back to the mother. It appeared that deprivation had enhanced the tie to the mother and rendered the contact-comfort need so prepotent that need for the mother overwhelmed the exploratory motives during the brief, three-minute test sessions. No change in these behaviors was observed throughout the 185-day period. When the mother was absent from the open field, the behavior of the infants was similar in the initial retention test to that during the preseparation tests; but they tended to show gradual adaptation to the open-field situation with repeated testing and, consequently, a reduction in their emotionality scores.

In the last five retention test periods, an additional test was introduced in which the surrogate mother was placed in the center of the room and covered with a clear Plexiglas box. The monkeys were initially disturbed and frustrated when their explorations and manipulations of the box failed to provide contact with the mother. However, all animals adapted to the situation rather rapidly. Soon they used the box as a place of orientation for exploratory and play behavior, made frequent contacts with the objects in the field, and very often brought these objects to the Plexiglas box. The emotionality index was slightly higher than in the condition of the available cloth mothers, but it in no way approached the emotionality level displayed when the cloth mother was absent. Obviously, the infant monkeys gained emotional security by the presence of the mother even though contact was denied.

Affectional retention has also been measured by tests in which the monkey must unfasten a three-device mechanical puzzle to obtain entrance into a compartment containing the mother surrogate. All the trials are initiated by allowing the infant to go through an unlocked door, and in half the trials it finds the mother present and in half, an empty compartment. The door is then locked and a ten-minute test conducted. In tests given prior to separation from the surrogate mothers, some of the infants had solved this puzzle and others had failed. On the last test before separation there were no differences in total manipulation under mother-present and mother-absent conditions, but striking differences exist between the two conditions throughout the post-separation test periods. Again, there is no interaction with conditions of feeding.

The over-all picture obtained from surveying the retention data is unequivocal. There is little, if any, waning of responsiveness to the mother throughout this five-month period as indicated by any measure. It becomes perfectly obvious that this affectional bond is highly resistant to forgetting and that it can be retained for very long periods of time by relatively infrequent contact reinforcement. During the next year, retention tests will be conducted at 90-day intervals, and further plans are dependent upon the results obtained. It would appear that affectional responses may show as much resistance to extinction as has been previously demonstrated for learned fears and learned pain, and such data would be in keeping with those of common human observation. . . .

We have already described the group of four control infants that had never lived in the presence of any mother surrogate and had demonstrated no sign of affection or security in the presence of the cloth mothers introduced in test sessions. When these infants reached the age of 250 days, cubicles containing both a cloth mother and a wire mother were attached to their cages. There was no lactation in these mothers, for the monkeys were on a solid-food diet. The initial reaction of the monkeys to the alterations was one of extreme disturbance. All the infants screamed violently and made repeated attempts to escape the cage whenever the door was opened. They kept a maximum distance from the mother surrogates and exhibited a considerable amount of rocking and crouching behavior, indicative of emotionality. Our first thought was that the critical period for the development of maternally directed affection had passed and that these macaque children were doomed to live as affectional orphans. Fortunately, these behaviors continued for only 12 to 48 hours and then gradually ebbed, changing from indifference to active contact on, and exploration of, the surrogates. The home-cage behavior of these control monkeys slowly became similar to that of the animals raised with the mother surrogates from birth. Their manipulation and play on the cloth mother became progressively more vigorous to the point of actual mutilation, particularly during the morning after the cloth mother had been given her daily change of terry covering. The control subjects were now actively running to the cloth mother when frightened and had to be coaxed from her to be taken from the cage for formal testing.

[We plotted] the amount of time these infants spent on the mother surrogates. Within 10 days mean contact time is approximately nine hours, and this measure remains relatively constant throughout the next 30 days. Consistent with the results on the subjects reared from birth with dual mothers, these late-adopted infants spent less than one and one-half hours per day in contact with the wire mothers, and this activity level was relatively constant throughout the test sessions. Although the maximum time that the control monkeys spent on the cloth mother was only about half that spent by the original dual mother-surrogate group, we cannot be sure that this discrepancy is a function of differential early experience. The control monkeys were about three months older when the mothers were attached to their cages than the experimental animals had been when their mothers were removed and the retention tests begun. Thus, we do not know what the amount of contact would be for a 250-day-old animal raised from birth with surrogate mothers. Nevertheless, the magnitude of the differences and the fact that the contact-time curves for the mothered-from-birth infants had remained constant for almost 150 days suggest that early experience with the mother is a variable of measurable importance.

The control group has also been tested for differential visual exploration after the introduction of the cloth and wire mothers. By the second test session a high level of exploratory behavior had developed, and the responsiveness to the wire mother and the empty box is significantly greater than that to the cloth mother. This is probably not an artifact since there is every reason to believe that the face of the cloth mother is a fear stimulus to most monkeys that have not had extensive experience with this object during the first 40 to 60 days of life. Within the third test session a sharp change in trend occurs, and the cloth mother is then more frequently viewed than the wire mother or the blank box; this trend continues during the fourth session, producing a significant preference for the cloth mother.

Before the introduction of the mother surrogate into the home-cage situation, only one of the four control monkeys had ever contacted the cloth mother in the open-field tests. In general, the surrogate mother not only gave the infants no security, but instead appeared to serve as a fear stimulus. The emotionality scores of these control subjects were slightly higher during the mother-present test sessions than during the mother-absent test sessions. These behaviors were changed radically by the fourth post-introduction test approximately 60 days later. In the absence of the cloth mothers the emotionality index in this fourth test remains near the earlier level, but the score is reduced by half when the mother is present, a result strikingly similar to that found for infants raised with the dual mother-surrogates from birth. The control infants now show increasing object exploration and play behavior, and they begin to use the mother as a base of operations, as did the infants raised from birth with the mother surrogates. However, there are still definite differences in the behavior of the two groups. The control infants do not rush directly to the mother and clutch her violently; but instead they go toward, and orient around, her, usually after an initial period during which they frequently show disturbed behavior, exploratory behavior, or both.

That the control monkeys develop affection or love for the cloth mother when she is introduced into the cage at 250 days of age cannot be questioned. There is every reason to believe, however, that this interval of delay depresses the intensity of the affectional response below that of the infant monkeys that were surrogate-mothered from birth onward. In interpreting these data it is well to remember that the control monkeys had had continuous opportunity to observe and hear other monkeys housed in adjacent cages and that they had had limited opportunity to view and contact surrogate mothers in the test situations, even though they did not exploit the opportunities.

During the last two years we have observed the behavior of two infants raised by their own mothers. Love for the real mother and love for the surrogate mother appear to be very similar. The baby macaque spends many hours a day clinging to its real mother. If away from the mother when frightened, it rushes to her and in her presence shows comfort and composure. As far as we can observe, the infant monkey's affection for the real mother is strong, but no stronger than that of the experimental monkey for the surrogate cloth mother, and the security that the infant gains from the presence of the real mother is no greater than the security it gains from a cloth surrogate. . . . But, whether the mother is real or a cloth surrogate, there does develop a deep and abiding bond between mother and child. In one case it may be the call of the wild and in the other the McCall of civilization, but in both cases there is "togetherness."

In spite of the importance of contact comfort, there is reason to believe that other variables of measurable importance will be discovered. Postural support may be such a variable, and it has been suggested that, when we build arms into the mother surrogate, 10 is the minimal number required to provide adequate child care. Rocking motion may be such a variable, and we are comparing rocking and stationary mother surrogates and inclined planes. The differential responsiveness to cloth mother and cloth-covered inclined plane suggests that clinging as well as contact is an affectional variable of importance. Sounds, particularly natural, maternal sounds, may operate as either unlearned or learned affectional variables. Visual responsiveness may be such a variable, and it is possible that some semblance of visual imprinting may develop in the neonatal monkey. There are indications that this becomes a variable of importance during the course of infancy through some maturational process.

John Bowlby has suggested that there is an affectional variable which he calls "primary object following," characterized by visual and oral search of the mother's face. Our surrogate-mother-raised baby monkeys are at first inattentive to her face, as are human neonates to human mother faces. But by 30 days of age ever-increasing responsiveness to the mother's face appears—whether through learning, maturation, or both—and we have reason to believe that the face becomes an object of special attention.

Our first surrogate-mother-raised baby had a mother whose head was just a ball of wood since the baby was a month early and we had not had time to design a more esthetic head and face. This baby had contact with the blank-faced mother for 180 days and was then placed with two cloth mothers, one motionless and one rocking, both being endowed with painted, ornamented faces. To our surprise the animal would compulsively rotate both faces 180 degrees so that it viewed only a round, smooth face and never the painted, ornamented face. Furthermore, it would do this as long as the patience of the experimenter in reorienting the faces persisted. The monkey showed no sign of fear or anxiety, but it showed unlimited persistence. Subsequently it improved its technique, compulsively removing the heads and rolling them into its cage as fast as they were returned. We are intrigued by this observation, and we plan to examine systematically the role of the mother face in the development of infant-monkey affections. Indeed, these observations suggest the need for a series of ethological-type researches on the two-faced female.

Although we have made no attempts thus far to study the generalization of infant-macaque affection or love, the techniques which we have developed offer promise in this uncharted field. Beyond this, there are few if any technical difficulties in studying the affection of the actual, living mother for the child, and the techniques developed can be utilized and expanded for the analysis and developmental study of father-infant and infant-infant affection.

Since we can measure neonatal and infant affectional responses to mother surrogates, and since we know they are strong and persisting, we are in a position to assess the effects of feeding and contactual schedules; consistency and inconsistency in the mother surrogates; and early, intermediate, and late maternal deprivation. Again, we have here a family of problems of fundamental interest and theoretical importance.

If the researches completed and proposed make a contribution, I shall be grateful; but I have also given full thought to possible practical applications. The socioeconomic demands of the present and the threatened socioeconomic demands of the future have led the American woman to displace, or threaten to displace, the American man in science and industry. If this process continues, the problem of proper child-rearing practices faces us with startling clarity. It is cheering in view of this trend to realize that the American male is physically endowed with all the really essential equipment to compete with the American female on equal terms in one essential activity: the rearing of infants. We now know that women in the working classes are not needed in the home because of their primary mammalian capabilities; and it is possible that in the foreseeable future neonatal nursing will not be regarded as a necessity, but as a luxury—to use Veblen's term—a form of conspicuous consumption limited perhaps to the upper classes. But whatever course history may take, it is comforting to know that we are now in contact with the nature of love.

IAN D. SUTTIE

The Biology of Love
and Interest, Etc.

Ian D. Suttie's The Origins of Love and Hate *was published (London: Kegan Paul) in 1935, and it was not until 1952 that I was able to persuade an American publisher to issue the book on this side of the Atlantic.[1] Having, like Suttie, been brought up in the Freudian tradition, I had passed through much of the same critical development as Suttie in seeing so much that was in error in Freud. Not that that diminished by one iota our great respect for the sheer intellectual achievement of Freud. A great man can afford to make errors, and the more fruitful they are the better. Great innovators are not well served when their teaching is converted into a cult and its followers spend their time forcing the facts to fit the theories, as psychoanalysts have done for more than half a century. It was, therefore, a tremendous experience for me to read Suttie's book. It is by all odds the finest criticism of Freudian theory, and at the same time the most original corrective contribution to psychoanalytic theory that we have to this day. I have chosen to reprint here the whole of chapter 1, with the exception of the opening paragraph.*

As the reader will immediately perceive, Suttie at once gets to the point: the fundamental importance of the mother in the development of the human being—a point that is elaborated throughout the book in the most illuminating and stimulating ways. His repeated statements concerning the caressing the child receives from the mother and the role this plays in his later development of friendships, and in the substitutes for caressing he enjoys in play and conversation, were the source of my own interest in touching and in the publication many years later of my book on the subject.[2] Suttie's book is full of such productive suggestions,

"The Biology of Love and Interest, Etc." by Ian D. Suttie. From *The Origins of Love and Hate* (New York: The Julian Press, Inc., 1952), pp. 15–21. Reprinted by permission of the publisher.

[1] The book is published in the United States, with an introduction by Ashley Montagu, by the Julian Press, Inc., New York, in both hardback and paperback editions.

[2] Ashley Montagu, *Touching: The Human Significance of the Skin.*

some of which he was himself in the process of developing when his early death ended his career. The Origins of Love and Hate *constitutes an enduring contribution to our understanding of love, hate, and human nature. It is hoped that this chapter from Suttie's book will send many readers to the complete work.*

Everyday life and mental illness alike are now regarded as an attempt to master anxiety, and this anxiety itself is no longer considered to be merely frustrated sexual desire but is regarded as largely due to hatred and aggressive wishes. The task of healthy development is even described by Dr. Brierly as "overcoming hatred with love," and, in many devious ways, psychoanalytic theory is recognizing more clearly the social nature of man and is no longer presenting his psychology as that of a self-contained entity independent of his fellows except insofar as his bodily appetites and gratifications demand their services. Psychoanalysis, in fact, is losing much that made it obnoxious to European philosophy, good sense and good feeling, but it still fails to take a wide enough view of its subject matter. This statement may seem outrageous to many who are acquainted with psychoanalytic studies of art, biography, primitive custom, etc., but it must be remembered that psychoanalytic ideas are merely *applied* in these fields; they are *developed* and *tested* almost exclusively in the consulting room.

From the widest scientific and philosophic standpoint, we must consider the human mind as the product of evolution—that is to say, as having had its definite function to serve in the survival of our species and in the attainment of our present dominant position. Later we shall find it necessary to consider mind from two other points of view also—namely as the result of the child's contact with members of its own family, and as the result of its parents' social and cultural relationships. The evolution of cultures and civilizations cannot be explained in terms of the individual minds which are its members. Nor should mind be considered in isolation from its social contacts. Psychologists are prone to describe a mind as if it were an independent self-contained but standardized entity, a number of which, grouped together in some mysterious way, constitutes a society. Anthropologists frequently make the opposite mistake and describe social organizations and behavior with little reference to the minds which produce and are molded by these institutions. The separation of the science of mind from that of society is arbitrary and was originally dictated by practical convenience and the tastes and fancy of the student. The two sciences must be pursued in relation to each other, for mind is social and society is mental. Finally, the whole study of human behavior must be correlated with that of the social animals both on the grounds of the evolutionary relationship of species and of the common purposes in life and the different means of attaining these.

We must first, then, direct our study to the relationship between the human mind and those of animals which *might be* similar to those of our remote ancestors. Formerly, comparative psychology was the play-ground of the Victorian armchair theorists who cheerfully attributed much of their own ill-understood mentality to the higher animals and even the social insects. Mind in those days was regarded as mainly concerned with the intelligent pursuit of rational purposes and/or with the instinctive performance of some biological task satisfying some need or *condition of survival.* Worse still, these old psychologists recon-structed the mind of the *infant* in terms of this false conception of *animal* mind. The child and primitive adults, they supposed, were alike and but a stage removed from our prehuman ancestors who, in turn, were regarded as very similar to the higher animals, although, as we shall see, the very opposite is the case. Accordingly, the infant's disposition was regarded as a bundle of instincts, some of which, like sex, remained latent till adult life (!), while others had to be disciplined and held in control by education and civilization.

If ever a doubt arose as to the forces which brought about this supposed *subjection of animal impulses,* one or other of three different explanations was offered.

- Religion and the will of God was cited, though it did not well explain *animal* society or the fact that primitive peoples conform far more closely and rigorously to tribal custom and moral codes than civilized Christians do.

- Reason and utility were popular as an alternative explanation; though here again it was difficult to understand how a species of animals like our presocial ancestors could foresee the advantage of social co-operation without culture or experience, could negotiate such a social contract without language, and could adhere to the bargain without moral impulses.

- A third type of explanation of man's social character suggested that a change had occurred in his inherited constitution; in other words, a chemical change in the germ plasm. According to this "herd instinct" theory, man is different from birth from nonsocial animals. The theory, however, really explains nothing and has been utterly useless, adding nothing to our knowledge and presenting an illusory solution to the problem. Further, it presents the difficulty of forcing us to suppose that the same variation has occurred in at least twenty-five different species of insects and in a very great number of species of birds and mammals; whereas man, the most social of all, has the greatest difficulty in maintaining his adjustment to social life.

It will be no matter for surprise that, with such conceptions of the infant mind and of the forces molding upbringing, no progress was made in the understanding either of the child or of society. Such conclusions as these early speculators arrived at were wrong in every material respect and wholly useless as working hypotheses for further investigation. When we actually study the facts of social life comparatively, in order to see if social differ from solitary animals in any respect *other than this habit,* the important fact emerges that social animals as a rule nurture their young and conversely that nurtured animals tend to be more or less social. The social disposition seems to be a modified continuance of the infant's need for the nurtural parent's presence (even when the material need is outgrown). Into it enters also nurtural or parental impulses, but there is no need to postulate a special social instinct.

We need in fact only suppose the child is born with a mind and instincts *adapted to infancy;* or, in other words, so disposed as to profit by parental nurture. This is not an unreasonable supposition, but it implies the conclusion that the child mind is *less* like that of primitive animals than is the adult mind. It is less like animal mind since it is adapted to a milieu and mode of behaving vastly different from that of free-living, self-supporting animals. Instead of an armament of instincts—latent or otherwise—which would lead it to attempt on its own account things impossible to its powers or even undesirable—it is born with a simple attachment to mother, who is the sole source of food and protection. Instincts of self-preservation, such as would be appropriate in an animal which has to fend for itself, would be positively destructive to the dependent infant, whose impulses *must* be adapted to its mode of livelihood, namely a pseudo-parasitism.

We can reject therefore once and for all the notion of the infant mind being a bundle of co-operating or competing instincts, and suppose instead that it is dominated from the beginning by the need to retain the mother—a need which, if thwarted, must produce the utmost extreme of terror and rage, since the loss of mother is, under natural conditions, but the precursor of death itself. We have now to consider whether this attachment to mother is merely the sum of the infantile bodily needs and satisfactions which refer to her, or whether the *need for a mother is primarily presented to the child mind as a need for company and as a discomfort in isolation.* I can see no way of settling this question conclusively, but the fact is indisputable that a need for company, moral encouragement, attention, protectiveness, leadership, etc., remains after all the sensory gratifications connected with the mother's body have become superfluous and have been surrendered. In my view this is a direct development of the primal attachment to mother, and, further, I think that play, co-operation, competition and culture interests generally are substitutes for the mutually caressing relationship of child and mother. *By these substitutes we put the whole social environment in the place once occupied by mother*—maintaining with it a mental or cultural rapport in lieu of the bodily relationship of caresses, etc., formerly enjoyed with the mother. A joint interest in *things* has replaced the reciprocal interest in *persons;* friendship has developed out of love. True, the personal love and sympathy is preserved in *friendship;* but this differs from love insofar as it comes about by the *direction of attention upon the same things* (rather than upon each other), or by the pursuit of *the same activities even if these are not intrinsically useful* and gratifying, as is the case with much ritual and dance, etc. The interest is intensified even if it is not entirely created (artificial) by being *shared;* while the fact of sharing interest deepens the appreciation of the other person's presence even while it deprives it of sensual (or better of sensorial) qualities.

This is my view of the process of sublimation; but it differs very greatly from that of Freud and his enormous team of expert specialists. As far as anyone can tell, Freud considers that all the infant's desires for the mother, and the gratification it receives from her, are of a sexual nature. Indeed, it is probable that a strict Freudian would define all pleasure or satisfaction as "sexual." These longings and urges are called "skin," "eye," "mouth" and other erotisms to indicate their essentially *sexual* nature. At a certain age, Freud tells us, they become organized under the supremacy of "the genital zone." That is to say they become "sexual" in the proper and popular meaning of the word. Having become sexual—according to Freud—they have also become incestuous (directed towards other members of the same family) and hence lead to jealousy. The Oedipus complex is thereby established. Undergoing repression next from fear of the rival's displeasure and revenge, these sexual wishes (for the parent of opposite sex) become goal-inhibited; that is to say, become a desexualized love. Or they may be deflected to the parent of the same sex, thereby constituting homosexuality, and then sublimated as friendship. The wishes them-selves may be altered, distorted or symbolized *beyond recognition*, and this "displacement" from the original biological objective is imagined as the basis of culture interest in the race and (presumably) of sublima-tion in the individual (Freud, *Introductory Lectures*, p. 290).

Freud's view seems to me inadequate to explain the mechanism of the development of interest or its very early appearance in childhood, that is to say, its appearance before the maturation, repression and sublimation of sexuality can be imagined to have taken place. Further, it is certain that the Freudian ideas in these matters cannot explain the constitution of society. Society, in fact, never was instituted by an aggregation of independent adult individuals, nor even by the growth of a single family by polygamy, group marriage, exogamy or otherwise. Society exists already in the group of the children of the same mother and develops by the addition of others to this original love group. Neither does culture arise by the thwarting of sex impulse and its deflection to symbolic ends (Freudian sublimation). Still less does it arise through rational cooperation in the pursuit of the material necessities of life. Necessity is not the mother of invention; play is.

Play is a necessity, not merely to develop the bodily and mental faculties, but to give to the individual that reassuring contact with his fellows which he has lost when the mother's nurtural services are no longer required or offered. Conversation is mental play, but it is long before the child completely outgrows the need for bodily contact. Even many adults retain the need for caresses apart from sexual intentions and gratifications. Nevertheless cultural interests do ultimately form a powerful antidote to loneliness even where there is no participator present in person; that is to say, cultural pursuits have a social value even where the other person is imagined or left unspecified.

We can now clearly understand why man has become virtually the only cultural animal and hence by far the most sociable. We can also understand from the same considerations why man has developed an aggressiveness, a competitiveness and a complex morality in which also he is unique. The neo-Freudians, approaching this point of view, no longer refer to human life as a struggle for pleasure, sense gratification or self-expression (detensioning) as formerly. They see the master motive of humanity as the "struggle to master anxiety" and further recognize this dread to be one of separation. Still, they endeavor to retain a materialistic, individualistic interpretation of separation anxiety; but, more and more, psychologists are convinced that it is really a dread of loneliness which is the *conscious expression of the human form of the instinct of self-preservation* which originally attached the infant to its mother.

It is as if the process of evolution had taken back with one hand a portion of the benefits conferred by the other. Man has to be thankful for

- his prolonged and sheltered immaturity, which provides leisure and a respite from the struggle for existence in which to *experiment* with development and with behavior;

- he has to thank the extreme plasticity of his instinct of *self-preservation* which originally attached the infant to his capacity to deflect interest from the satisfaction of appetite and from the procuring of defense and the means of existence, to activities we call cultural, which, in turn, have *incidentally* procured for him a tremendous mastery over all nature except his own. Against these benefits (of the opportunity to develop and to learn and the interest disposition to do so) we must set the very equivocal power to love and the need for love. While this provides the incentive and conditions for *learning* by experience and for accumulating knowledge from generation to generation and so of building up an immortal tradition, at the same time it drives man so hard as to make him anxious, aggressive and inhibited. Man is the only *anxious* animal. When nature produced him, she found herself with an explosive on her hands which she did not know how to handle. For all our language, cultural achievements and our family life, our love need is still seeking new techniques of social relationship. In this search for the security and satisfaction of social integration (fellowship), we are constantly driven into false channels which we will have to study presently.

To sum up the evolutionary antecedents of man, we may say the principal features that distinguish him from other (even social) animals are:

- the extreme degree to which the definite, stereotyped, specific, instincts of self-preservation of his prehuman ancestors are melted down or unfocused into a dependent love for mother, which, in turn, becomes need for others and finally parental love and interest, social feeling, etc.

- the prolongation of the period of immaturity between organically nurtured infancy and matehood and parenthood. This, as I said, along with the social need, affords both the opportunity and the incentive to co-operative activities not concerned with the material necessities of existence, and which may therefore develop indefinitely on free *playful* and *experimental* lines. The organic bodily relationships of infancy, matehood and parenthood can be imagined as affording security and satiety to this social need, and in them, moreover, the interest of each party is absorbed in the other *person* rather than directed upon things and *joint pursuits*. Further, adulthood has its practical, material cares that demand close attention to business and the rigorous adherence to well-tried customary methods of getting things done. The practical man is notoriously stereotyped—a creature of habit and opposed to all innovation. Practical shipbuilders told us a century ago that iron ships could not float. We can therefore conclude that the period of *youth* is not only that of mental development in the individual, but is the reason for the development of that distinctively human product, culture.

- the fact (mentioned [earlier]) that in man a collection of instincts is replaced by a relatively aimless and plastic curiosity, attachments and interest, is of course the reason why this play period can be turned to such account. Nonappetitive interest combined with need-for-company (they may even have the same origin) apply the drive to the cultural pursuits of knowledge for its own sake and to the development of a tradition which can be accumulated indefinitely.

These three characteristics then represent the advantages that the course of evolution has conferred upon man. Respectively they make him *social, educable* and *progressive.* At the same time evolution has left man with so little definite biological guidance in the form of instinct and with so much drive towards association and experiment that he has become *unstable and pervertible.* Other distinctively human characteristics are thus accounted for, namely man's anxiety, his arbitrary social customs and his liability to psychogenic mental disorder. Now we can see why man has been set a peculiar task which to some seems to offset his advantages—namely the task of understanding and mastering himself. This is what gives to modern psychology its peculiar importance and makes it a matter of urgency that it should be widely and critically studied by every citizen and not relegated to the specialist.

Having presented a synoptical picture of the fundamentals of human nature as I see it, it is, therefore, only fair to show how this compares with the broad outlines of the Freudian view. The difference will be found to turn largely, but by no means wholly, on the meaning attached to the word sexual.

I see in the infant's longing for the mother an expression of what in free-living animals we call the "self-preservative" instinct. Consistently with this, I see in anxiety and hate an expression of apprehension or discomfort at the frustration, or threatened frustration, of this all-important motive. Freud sees the infantile attachment as sexual and indeed sensual, while he regards anxiety and hate as proceeding from a separate independent instinct for destruction *which even aims to destroy its possessor.* The latter theory of death instinct has produced the greatest dissensions in the ranks of psychoanalysts themselves, and has been shown to be completely untenable and self-contradictory in many ways.

Again the period between infancy and adulthood appears to me to be dominated by an almost insatiable social need, which uses the plastic energy of human interest for its satisfaction in play. Freud sees this period as one of repression of the (by now definitely *genital*) sex impulses on account of their incestuous aims. Interest for Freud is just a substitute for, *or sublimation* of, sexual yearnings, and friendship is sexuality which has become *"goal-inhibited"* by the definitely genital wish becoming repressed. He accounts for the supposed stronger cultural drive in the male sex on the supposition that the Oedipus wish (sexual desire for mother) is stronger and better repressed than is the girl's corresponding desire for her father. It seems to me that man's cultural need is greater than woman's, inasmuch as he can never look forward to the bodily functions of maternity and lactation by which evolution has conferred upon women the virtual monopoly of the child. In a later chapter I will deal with the evidence of this and other jealousies which are much neglected by Freudians.

Further comparison of views must be deferred until after a consideration of the subjective aspect of the infant's mind.

The Biology of Hate and Anxiety

In organisms which are not born in a state of nurtural dependency the emotion of anger is little more than an intensification of effort to overcome frustration. Anger and fear are thus closely akin in their function as in their physiological mechanism, the former aiming to attain an end, the latter to avoid a danger.

I am suggesting that, in animals born or hatched in a state of nurtural dependency, the whole instinct of self-preservation, including the potential dispositions to react with anger and fear, is at first directed towards the mother. Anger is then aimed, not at the direct removal of frustration or attainment of the goal of the moment, still less at her destruction, but *at inducing the mother to accomplish these wishes for the child.* Instead of being the most desperate effort at *self-help* it has become the most insistent demand upon the *help of others*—the most emphatic plea which cannot be overlooked. It is now the maximal effort to *attract* attention, and as such must be regarded as a protest against unloving conduct rather than as aiming at destruction of the mother, which would have fatal repercussions upon the self.

Hatred, I consider, is just a standing reproach to the hated person, and owes all its meaning to a demand for love. If it were a desire (or appetite for destruction for its own sake), I cannot see how it could be focused so definitely upon one individual and as a rule upon a person who is significant in the subject's life. I would say "Earth hath no hate *but* love to hatred turned, and hell no fury but a baby scorned," for hatred, except for a preferred rival or a rejecting lover, does not seem to exist. At bottom therefore hatred is always ambivalent, always self-frustrated. It has no free outlet, can look for no favorable response, and this is why it is so important in psychopathology.[1]

In the same way the instinct of fear must be modified to suit the conditions of nurtured infancy. The helpless infant cannot flee or perform any avoiding reactions efficiently, so that the emotion of fear can find useful expression *only as an appeal to the mother.* As in the case of anger, the response expected and desired is not an identical emotion on the part of the mother. Either anger or apprehension on her part increases the corresponding disturbance in the child's mind. Where the child is afraid, it is reassured by her confidence and serenity, but not by her indifference and neglect, which is perhaps the worst of all for the child. Neglect of the fear appeal is extremely traumatic.

---

[1] In a measure it must undergo *automatic inhibition,* or repression, and this process is already being dimly perceived by clinical analysis.

M. BEVAN-BROWN

The Sources of Love and Fear

In this contribution, drawn from his work, The Sources of Love and Fear *(1950), Dr. Bevan-Brown draws attention to the importance of maternal love, especially in the breast-feeding situation, and particularly during the first year. Everything we have learned since his book was published has fully confirmed his views, which were based on years of observation and study at The Tavistock Clinic in London and in practice in New Zealand. At this late date well over 90 percent of women in the United States do not breast-feed their babies, and many of them can hardly be said to know how to love them. In the developing countries, such as those of Africa, mothers are following the European example and bottle-feeding their babies, with most unfortunate effects.*[1]

It is gravely to be doubted whether one may speak of a maternal instinct in the human species, as Dr. Bevan-Brown does. But one thing is certain: whatever biological predispositions there may be in women at childbirth and afterwards to mother their infants, a great deal of learning enters into such maternal behavior.[2] *The evidence strongly indicates that much of that learning is acquired from the manner in which the future mother has herself been mothered.*[3]

Without actually using the term, Dr. Bevan-Brown underscores the importance of unconditional love as contrasted with the "ifs" and "buts" of conditional love. He is also one of the few students of human nature who recognize the great damage that the doctrine of original sin has done, especially when applied by mothers to their infants. Also, he gets to the point at once—namely, that the human neonate is extremely immature at birth, "an embryo," so to speak, and therefore requires

"The Sources of Love and Fear" by Dr. M. Bevan-Brown. From *The Sources of Love and Fear* (New York: Vanguard Press, Inc., 1950), pp. 10–21. Copyright © 1950 by M. Bevan-Brown. Reprinted by permission of Vanguard Press, Inc.

[1] Nicholas Wade, "Bottle-Feeding: Adverse Effects of a Western Technology," *Science*, 184 (1974), 45–48; A. Berg, *The Nutrition Factor* (Washington, D.C.: The Brookings Institute, 1973).

[2] John Bowlby, *Child Care and the Growth of Love* (Baltimore: Penguin Books, 1953); Sylvia Brody, *Patterns of Mothering* (New York: International Universities Press, 1956).

[3] Harriet L. Rheingold, ed., *Maternal Behavior in Mammals* (New York: John Wiley & Sons, 1963); Harry H. Harlow, *Learning to Love* (New York: Ballantine Books, 1971).

much tender loving care. Here Bevan-Brown approaches very closely the editor's view of the human newborn as an exterogestate *who has only half completed his gestation in the womb.*[4]

On the damage almost invariably done to the young child when it goes to hospital and is separated from the mother, Bevan-Brown was also ahead of his time. It was as a result of his work at the Tavistock Clinic that the first proofs of this were published.[5]

Dr. Bevan-Brown may be quite right about circumcision, but at the present time nothing is quite resolved, even though a strong case has been made against the operation.[6]

Finally, the author's discussion of the importance of breast-feeding underscores once again the importance of this experience for the development of a loving human being.

The first thing that the psychiatrist has to make known is that if he seeks to bring about a radical cure of his patients, he has to investigate with the patient crucial experiences of the earliest years of the patient's life. The earliest years are obviously the years 1 to 3. It is within these three years that most of the experiences occur which are the source of an illness appearing ten, twenty or thirty years later. Furthermore, as a result of this work the evidence is continually increasing to show that the first year, and especially what should be the breast-feeding period, is the most important of all.

To the ordinary person who has never investigated the matter and has various common assumptions about the nature of these disorders, these facts seem startling and even incredible. But suppose he is reasonable enough to keep an open mind about the matter and then reflects upon it. It is obvious that a child's mother is, or should be, the first person in the world with whom he associates. She represents the first *personal* relationship, the first *social* relationship, the first *sensuous* relationship, the first *love* relationship. Without any technical knowledge of the subject, it would be reasonable to assume that this

[4] See Ashley Montagu, "The Origin and Significance of Neonatal Immaturity in Man," *Journal of the American Medical Association*, 178 (1961), 156–57. Reprinted in Ashley Montagu, ed., *Culture and Human Development* (Englewood Cliffs, N.J.: Prentice-Hall Inc., 1974), pp. 29–33.

[5] James Robertson, *Young Children in Hospital* (London: Tavistock Institute Publications Ltd., 1958); James Robertson, *A Two-Year-Old Goes to Hospital: A Scientific Film Record* (London: Tavistock Publications Ltd., 1953).

[6] E. Noel Preston, "Whither the Foreskin? A Consideration of Routine Neonatal Circumcision," *Journal of the American Medical Association*, 213 (1970), 1853–58.

relationship, being the first, sets the pattern of all subsequent relationships. That is, of course, supposing he is prepared to grant that the baby in the first year has primitive means of awareness of the existence of another person and is not merely an animated lump of protoplasm! Whether inferred or not, it is this principle that the psychiatrist finds to be true by cumulative evidence, derived from the emotional history of his patients. The word "history" here must not be misunderstood. The patients themselves have of course no memory of these early years, and if they are told at the beginning of their treatment that the sources of their troubles lie in these years, they tend to be as incredulous as anyone else. A long and arduous investigation into matters previously unconscious is necessary. At the end of a successful treatment, however, they have a feeling of conviction about the importance of their earlier experiences which is most interesting to observe. It is an inner conviction based on living experiences, and even the physician, supposing he wished to do so, would not be able to shake it. We have used this word "experiences" frequently and the reader may be impatient to learn what kind of experience is implied here which is so fateful for later life. *All the experiences involve situations in which the child was ignored, rejected, undervalued, disapproved of, scolded, punished, frustrated, discouraged, intimidated or frightened by the mother,* or perhaps by some other person who is taking the place of the mother and frequently should not be doing so.

Having indicated the conditions which tend towards neurosis, we must now consider the opposite question, namely what are the conditions tending towards health? They can be summed up in one short sentence: "The child must be loved, and especially by the mother." To many this will seem a platitude: many also will say that the vast majority of mothers do love their children. Now investigation shows that not all mothers do in fact love their children in the sense that is required; though they may be firmly convinced that they do. It can be shown that it is only a minority of mothers who do love their children in the sense that is required. They are not necessarily to blame for this: many of them with the best will in the world are not capable of such an attitude without expert help. As regards the question of platitude—to say "The child must be loved" is easy, but to explain what this means is less easy. We must embark upon this task. "Loving" includes "liking," "valuing," "respecting," "protecting," "enjoying," and transcends all these.

It may fairly be assumed that in humans, as well as in many animals, love of parent (especially mother) for offspring is naturally based upon instinct; in other words we may legitimately talk of "maternal instinct." If it is true that many humans do not love their offspring adequately, then they must be disabled in some way: there must be forces at work interfering with the free operation of this instinct. It would be foolish and futile to announce such an apparent platitude as "The child must be loved" without indicating some of the factors or forces interfering with the development and operation of maternal love.

First then it is the *child* that must be loved, objectively, that is to say, as he is, both physically and mentally, without reserve, without "ifs" and "buts." And this applies from the first hour—even minutes—of extra-uterine life. If so then it is clearly necessary to know what kind of creature a baby is. For on this matter various rather arbitrary opinions have been held. By some he has been regarded as an angel direct from heaven (i.e. not human); by others as liable to become a little devil unless precautions in the form of "discipline" are taken; by others still, a lump of animated protoplasm with no particular feelings except an appetite. Some, on the basis of a quasi-religious outlook, regard him as a fallen creature, or as having been born in sin, and therefore actually or potentially bad or sinful. If the mother holds any of these views as to the nature of the child, her relationship with him is liable to be disastrous. For example, if she regards him as potentially bad, it will be impossible for her to love him adequately in the sense in which we are using that word, for then she must needs alter, correct or "improve" him. We shall refer to the effects of this policy later; but the first is of course that the child feels unloved but is quite incapable of understanding why.

It is perhaps important to mention here another common and insidious fallacy. The child during the first decade or even up to puberty is not a miniature adult and to assume that he is this is both unjust and dangerous. He is no more a miniature adult than a cotyledon is a miniature tree. This difficulty, however, usually arises with children from two years and upwards, and not in infancy.

The Baby Is a Person

What then is the nature of the infant? At birth he closely resembles the offspring of the higher mammals. He differs from these in two respects (1) his extreme helplessness and (2) in his potentiality—what he may become if he is well nurtured. *He is an embryo,* a going concern, a dynamic organism, a person, and a potential personality. He is a bundle of forces, psychic in nature, which are as yet primitive, autonomous, unintegrated, unco-ordinated and uncontrolled. There is as yet no "I," or ego, or personality to organize or control them. He has emerged into a noisy world from an intra-uterine situation where he was in complete equilibrium; and he needs the greatest care to help him through this violent and relatively sudden change.

First Need—Security

He is very prone to fear. This proneness of the infant to fear is of the utmost importance in early life. It must be constantly watched for, and he must be protected against it. To be exposed to fear is unquestionably the greatest psychic danger of the child in the first year. In the second year when he can to some extent fend for himself, the danger is less, though still present. It is remarkable and perhaps significant of the immaturity of our culture that so many people, even so many mothers, fail to realize the proneness of the infant to fear, and even tend to doubt the fact when it is pointed out. I have actually seen it stated in a standard text-book of academic psychology that a young infant does not experience much fear! Such adults will naïvely suppose that because they apprehend no danger and see no reason for fear that therefore the child should feel just as they do; and that, as there is in fact no danger from the adult point of view, it is stupid for him to fear and irritating if he cries. At this point I should like to refer to a little book, *Baby's Point of View*, by Joyce Partridge, an English surgeon and psychiatrist, published by Oxford Medical Publications. This little book is the most valuable I know regarding infant welfare and the author is admirably qualified as an authority. She gives a set of rules, one of which is "Never leave a baby (in the first year) alone to cry." This is an absolute rule: it does not say "pick the baby up every time he cries" nor does it forbid this if necessary: but it does say that while crying he must not be left alone. He may be crying because he is hungry, cold, too hot, wet, etc.; if so, these things may be attended to. But he may be none of these things: he may be crying because he is frightened, and if not reassured early this is a dangerous condition. It should be realized that the young baby is the most helpless creature in organic nature; he is utterly dependent, and he needs not only food, oxygen and water but also human association. The realization that his mother is there (when awake) or will always come if he needs her gives him a feeling of security, protection and confidence. Thus under these conditions he may never fall into fear at all. In the absence of such protection he certainly will do so; and the fear he then experiences is much more devastating than the type of fear the adult normally experiences: it is all-pervading panic—because he is quite unable to understand the situation, to fight it, or to run away: he can only wait for someone else to deal with it. Thus the first need of the infant is *security* which he derives from constant association with his mother. If the mother realizes this need and meets it in the earliest weeks, the child acquires a feeling of security and confidence in the mother which will enable him to meet emergencies without undue disturbance. If it is not met he will become an anxious child and may continue for months to cry immediately he is left. There has recently existed a school of infant nurture which has held the view that it is good to let the baby cry and leave him alone, that, since there is no (adult) danger, he must learn that it is stupid to cry. They suggest that this is the way to teach him self-reliance, and even that it is wrong to go to him when he cries because he is doing it on purpose to annoy or dominate his environment! This doctrine is not only very foolish but also pernicious and dangerous. Psychiatrists can all produce cases to show that it has laid the foundation for a permanent anxiety state in later life. Those who are familiar with the characteristics of an anxiety state will realize that it has all the characteristics of the panic of the infant: it is irrational, it is about everything or nothing in particular, it can neither be fought nor escaped from, it is all-pervading. The baby must not be left alone to cry. This, then, is the first principle of child nurture which we learn from the treatment of people suffering from emotional disorders; and if an infant in the early weeks and months of life is allowed to remain frightened and alone, this experience may be the origin of an anxiety state which may persist into adult life. There is nothing especially surprising about such a statement; the child's first impressions of the world into which he has come are that it is inhospitable, dangerous and lonely; and it is no use seeking help. He must try to fend for himself and not expect help; but he cannot fend for himself, he is helpless. It is not a matter for surprise that such impressions may colour his view of the world and the people in it permanently. Much of his subsequent conduct will be devoted to the object of making himself as secure as he can in an insecure world. (Incidentally it will follow that if there is a large proportion of such individuals in a nation they will tend to assume that other nations have hostile intentions towards them, and will concentrate on national security as well as personal security.) But there is a further reason why these early impressions become permanent attitudes. The child, being unable to reason or compare, does not proceed to consider that his mother is not perhaps as competent a person as she might be, and therefore not an adequate mother in that she does not comfort him; but he early begins to feel (not think) that the reason for this neglect is that he himself is valueless, worthless, insignificant, possibly bad in some way; therefore, in order to be loved and valued he will have to alter himself in some way or another. Here is the beginning of emotional conflict and repression; and the feelings of anxiety become involved with feelings of inferiority and guilt. If these dangers are to be avoided, the infant must be in close association with the mother for the first hours, days, weeks of life, so that whenever he wakes he has the feeling that she is near. Such an association makes the closest possible approximation to his intra-uterine security and placental attachment, which has just been broken. If this transition period is managed in this way for the first month or six weeks, the infant will acquire confidence in his environment and will soon be willing to lie awake alone in his cot without fear. We could well learn some lessons in motherhood from the behaviour of some of the higher mammals. We are inclined to consider that we are much superior as human beings to the higher mammals, but observation will show that some human mothers are inferior, as mothers, to the higher mammals.

Operations

While on the subject of security, we must refer to operations.

However skilfully managed, these are liable to be terrifying experiences to the child. The special danger is that usually the child is separated from his mother. Analytical treatment frequently reveals the feeling that she has wilfully or callously deserted him in his greatest need. From the point of view of prophylaxis it is important to avoid all operations except to save life before the age of four or five. The danger is less after this age, when the situation can be explained to the child. If an operation must be done it is important that the child be not separated from his mother.

Circumcision

It is extraordinary that in our day this rather barbaric rite should be practised almost as a routine with infants. From the psychological point of view it is dangerous with or without an anaesthetic. In the rare case where a child cannot urinate it may be done, but it is otherwise unjustifiable. Apparently the practice is based on a morbid fear of masturbation, and is unconsciously propitiatory. When performed at the age of two or three it is frequently the basis of severe castration fears.

Second Need—Sensuousness

We must now consider the second great need of the infant. But when we say "second" we do not mean secondary in importance. In the first place we will call this need *nutrition.* This word usually refers to a physiological need, but we hope to indicate that this is only a part of the nutritive need of the child. There are systems of infant welfare which start from the assumption that if a baby receives a certain proportion of protein, fat, carbohydrate and minerals, water and vitamins, at regular intervals, if he is kept warm and has napkins changed periodically then all will be well with him.

This assumption means that he in all respects resembles an engine or a piece of mechanism, or is in no respect different from a calf or lamb. If this assumption were correct it would be sound policy, as is so often recommended, to provide these substances through a bottle or a tube, thus avoiding what is regarded as the exacting task of breast-feeding. It is the duty of the psychiatrist to point out that this doctrine is false and that it is responsible for a host of troubles which continue into adult life, but which are never connected with their actual source. *The baby at birth is a person* and not a machine, and, being a person, has a need for close association with another person. And this person must have certain feelings and attitudes towards him, of which we shall have more to say presently. At the moment we will mention only that this person must be conscious and sentient. Before attempting to explain this matter further, we must draw attention to a principle which is important both biologically and psychologically and which underlies the whole matter.

We belong to a race of organisms which is the result of a long process of evolution. In common with all our ancestors, both mammalian and pre-mammalian, we are endowed with a very strong instinct tending towards intimate association with another individual. We can call this instinct or tendency a copulative tendency. Unfortunately the word "copulation" has been limited to the mechanical aspect of the reproductive act. The term has a much wider application than this and we are using it in that larger sense. This copulative tendency is to be observed in creatures as far back as the protozoa and it is true that in the more primitive organism it usually subserves reproduction. In the mammals and in man this copulative tendency is of supreme importance in the first months of life. We are here seeking to point out that the infant has an urgent need to copulate with a person, to wit, the mother, through the medium of the nipple and the mouth; and this need transcends the mere need for chemical sustenance. Clearly here this copulative process still subserves reproduction in that it has to do with the nurture of the infant, but it is a function of organs that are not commonly regarded as genital or reproductive. If we now pass from biological language to psychological language, and speak in human terms, we could say baldly that the infant requires love as well as milk. What the psychiatrist has discovered by a generation of labour is that even though the infant be provided with all the chemical substances necessary, at regular intervals in correct quantity, he may not thrive: he may thrive physically to a degree, while as a *personality* he may fail to thrive: but he may even in these circumstances fail to thrive physically. We are evidently drawn to the conclusion that if a child is to thrive mentally and physically he needs to be breast-fed, and this proposition can be made with confidence: *There are risks attaching to the development of any baby that has the misfortune not to be breast-fed.*

Quality of Breast-feeding

But even this conclusion needs further elaboration. Even though the baby may be breast-fed in the mechanical sense, and obtain milk from his mother of the correct chemical quality and quantity, he may still not thrive. Thus we come to the crux of the matter and the truth we hope to convey: unless this breast-feeding process is a true human copulation, that is to say, unless it is a mutual reciprocal and personal act as well as a mechanical process, the baby may not thrive. Again, it may be more explicitly stated that the breast-feeding must not be only chemical and physical but a *love relationship* if the baby is to thrive.

We must endeavour to explain what a love relationship is. The essential requirement here is that the mother enjoy this breast-feeding association and enjoy the baby in it, and also that the baby know that the mother is so enjoying it and him. It will at once be asked how possibly could a baby of one month old have any such knowledge or perception. I do not think I can give a convincing proof that the baby arrives at this perception; but I know that he has this ability; and this can be confirmed from the evidence of that select body of mothers who have fully performed the breast-feeding function. The evidence that I have from patients who are reproducing these experiences in the course of treatment of emotional disorders indicates that the sensuous experiences of the baby at the breast include the following components:

1. Intense sensations derived from contact of lips, tongue and palate with the nipple.
2. Sensations from contact of nose and cheek with the breast.
3. General sensations of softness and warmth.
4. Sensations of being enfolded, supported and held or embraced.
5. Bodily odours from the mother.
6. Sensations of satisfaction in mouth, pharynx, oesophagus and stomach of receiving warm milk.
7. Sounds of appropriate quality made by the mother.
8. Sensations in the hands of caressing, squeezing and patting the breast.
9. (not in the earlier weeks). Sight impressions of the mother's facial expression.

As regards (1) it should be noted that a young baby is "all mouth"; his mouth is paramount and his whole being is centred and focussed in it, the muscles surrounding the mouth being already strong and well-adapted for activity. It is to be expected, then, that the physical condition of the nipple during the process of breast-feeding is of vital importance—its size, its tension, its firmness, its elasticity, its vitality, its smoothness and response to the stimulus of sucking. It is very illuminating to learn from adult patients vivid details of such impressions; though as a rule these are the conditions of the nipple they are yearning for but not experiencing. It is necessary to add that many of these patients are adult males who know (intellectually) nothing about the matter and have had (since infancy) no such experience. These complaints (given under great stress) are of smallness (they cannot get hold of it), dryness, roughness, lifelessness, flaccidity, lack of response, etc. Sometimes they have a great feeling of frustration which they attribute to not being allowed to fondle the breast with their hands (their hands and arms being presumably wrapped up).

Another distressing feeling commonly reported is one of anxiety—there is an impression that they must hurry, the mother is rather impatient because she is busy and has other things to do and therefore must get this business over: therefore there is the feeling that the breast may be taken away before the child is satisfied. The point is that he never will be satisfied under these conditions: he wants and needs a love response from the mother and will go on sucking more and more frantically in the hope of getting it. This may lead to vomiting and distress, etc.

Returning then to the problem—how does the baby know that his mother is enjoying the breast-feeding situation and him in it (or not) and is therefore in fact loving him? My own conviction about this is that it is chiefly through the medium of component (1) (see above) i.e. from his perception of the condition and response of the nipple through sensations in lips, tongue, palate and pharynx.

Love and Duty

We live in a culture in which duty is regarded as a very high ideal. A mother may say that she regards it as her highest duty to breast-feed her child, but cannot by any means bring herself to really enjoy the process, and hence her breast-feeding is a sacrifice of herself. This would seem a very high and essentially human motive. But unfortunately such a motive is inadequate here. The astonishing fact is that the baby has the means of knowing that the mother is feeding him merely from a sense of duty, and he will feel unwanted, unloved, and experience consequent reactions of depression, fear, rage, etc. The inevitable conclusion is that in the nurture of the young at least, duty as a motive is inferior to love, and love involves not sacrifice of oneself to another person but *enjoyment of that person.*

We mentioned that fear is one of the reactions likely to occur in the situation we have described; that is, where the mother feeds the baby from a sense of duty and not enjoyment. Clearly this links up with the primary need that we discussed earlier, that of security. In fact, the need for security is intimately connected with this need for sensuous love which we have indicated. The two are inseparable in actual experience though it is convenient to consider them separately for purposes of description.

We have introduced a word here, *"sensuous"* which we used earlier and without explanation.

Freud and his followers have used the word "sexual" in this connection, viz., to refer to that type of feeling experienced by both the mother and the infant in this copulative breast-feeding process. We think that the use of this word "sexual" has led to confusion, and much prefer the word "sensuous." Some people, particularly mothers, describe this as "physical" enjoyment.

This leads us to draw attention to another principle, viz., that all healthy, vital and biological functions are attended by sensuousness or, if you like, pleasure or enjoyment. Such processes are eating, drinking, micturition, defaecation, breast-feeding, parturition, coitus, bathing, singing, dancing, muscular activity.

It is evident, then, that this sensuousness or enjoyment which should be experienced by both parties in the breast-feeding situation subserves *nutrition:* that which accompanies coitus, and which may more appropriately be called sexual, subserves *reproduction.* From the point of view of mental hygiene, which is our concern, the essential conclusion is that the subsequent physical and mental health of any individual depends very largely on whether or not he has experienced a true biological and psychological relationship with his mother in the first months of life, i.e. on whether he has been loved as an infant by his mother in a completely human sense.

BROCK CHISHOLM

The Need for Love

Brock Chisholm was a major general in the medical corps of the Canadian Army and president of the World Federation for Mental Health from 1948 to 1953. One of the valuable features of Chisholm's contribution to this text is that it draws attention to the tragic imitation of alleged Western virtues by the peoples of the so-called underdeveloped countries. In slavish imitation of the West, mothers almost everywhere in the world are giving up breast-feeding for the seeming advantages of bottle-feeding, with the most unfortunate results.[1] The relationship of breast-feeding and learning the experience of love, both for mother and *child, does not seem to be understood by most of our "authorities." As Chisholm suggests, we, in fact, would do well to copy some of the customs of "underdeveloped" peoples. The error of producing a wholly unwarranted sense of sin in the child is succinctly analyzed by Chisholm in this reading, as is "the mother-knows-best" syndrome.*

We cannot help concluding that adults are often deteriorated children who are much in need of tender loving care.

We know more now than we used to about the kinds of things that handicap children's development, and we know what the needs of children are. If a small child is given sufficient food and sufficient shelter, sufficient water or moisture to stay alive, the next requirement is love; close, warm, physical-contact love.

The time has gone when psychologists and psychiatrists blushed when they used the word "love." Love has now become a scientific term (which makes it respectable) and is now recognized as a good thing. Indeed, it is now considered indispensable, or nearly so, in early childhood for effective emotional development toward maturity.

"The Need for Love" (editor's title). From Brock Chisholm, *Prescription for Survival* (New York: Columbia University Press, 1957), pp. 37–48. Reprinted by permission of the publisher.

[1] Nicholas Wade, "Bottle-Feeding: Adverse Effects of a Western Technology," *Science*, 184 (1974), 45–48; A. Berg, *The Nutrition Factor* (Washington, D.C.: The Brookings Institution, 1973).

In this area, in our wonderfully advanced North America, we, oddly enough, are behind certain other cultures when it comes to loving our babies. We have acquired some rather dreadful habits—all in the name of Hygiene.

I am reminded of the time, some years ago, when I was in Pakistan, and was being guided through a very large general hospital. As we were going along a corridor, which was a sort of balcony on the side of the building, we passed the screened door to a ward. Suddenly someone pointed out to me, with great enthusiasm, something away off on the horizon in the opposite direction. Now, to any old Army inspecting officer, the situation was perfectly clear; there was something nearby they didn't want me to see. Therefore I was quite sure that whatever was hidden behind this screened door I should see. If you see only what people want you to see you will never find out anything.

So I insisted, at some risk of offense, on seeing this ward, and when I insisted, my guides began apologizing, saying that I wouldn't really like to see it at all. It was of a very old pattern; they were ashamed of it; they hoped to get it changed; they hoped that the World Health Organization might help them get the money to adopt modern and new patterns for this particular ward, because it was very bad indeed. It was a pattern hundreds of years old.

However, I still insisted that even as an antiquity I would like to see it. I went in to see this ward, with the reluctant accompaniment of the train of people with me, and I saw the best maternity ward I have ever seen in any country, far better than any I have ever seen in North America. Here was a big maternity ward with beds down both sides. The foot posts of each bed were extended up about three feet or so, and slung between the foot posts was a cradle. The baby was in the cradle, and I noticed as I looked down the ward that one squeak out of the baby and up would come the mother's foot, and with her toe she would rock the cradle. On the second squeak, which showed that the baby was really awake, she would reach into the cradle and take the baby into her arms, where a baby is supposed to be most of the time.

They wanted to get rid of that perfectly beautiful arrangement, to put their babies under glass the way we do, and to keep them in inspection wards where they can be seen at a distance by their loving fathers whenever they visit, and taken to their mother if she is good and does as the nurse tells her! They wanted to do all that because we Westerners had given them the impression that all our methods are superior to theirs.

Those babies, if they develop an infection, recover from it twice as fast as ours do. These people are not producing little neurotic babies of one month old the way we are. Their babies do not feel themselves out in the cold world, do not feel that nobody loves them from the moment they are born, as many of ours do. Mothers in that part of the world regard as perfectly savage some of the customs they have heard about in North America where mothers actually take their babies to hospitals, leave them there, and go home. No mother in Southeast Asia would do such a thing. She would fight everybody in the hospital before she would leave her baby there and go home without it. And she is right, demonstrably right.

Whenever a baby comes to a hospital in that part of the world, the mother accompanies it, and does everything for the baby that the baby needs that doesn't require the services of a trained nurse or of a physician. The baby feels at home all the time and recovers from operation or disease much faster than ours do, and does not suffer from any neurotic disabilities as the result of illness, as ours do.

I am not suggesting that we copy all of the patterns of these other countries. We need to be discriminating about other people's customs as well as our own, but we can learn a great deal about human relations, about the upbringing of children, from these other people. Whenever we become humble enough to learn with discrimination from others' experiments in living, we will begin to progress more steadily than we are now. Unfortunately we tend to regard our own living patterns as fixed and final and of universal value and so we naturally think everyone should copy us. This is just not true.

I have been discussing the small child's need for love as a primary condition of his effective development. Any threat to love, any risk of loss of love, is for a child a nightmare, a threatening barrier between him and his continuing exploration of life. Yet, very many children run into the threat of loss of love very early in life, sometimes even within the first year. Whenever a child behaves in ways that are not acceptable to the ideas, attitudes, and moral codes of his parents (particularly of his mother), he risks running into active disapproval. This is interpreted by the child as a threat of loss of love.

The very young child is not concerned at all with the local behavior customs of the natives; he is born not knowing anything about them. One can call him uncivilized, born in sin, or just not grown up; they are all the same thing. He is a "natural," born the way he is born. And, furthermore, there are no laws anywhere saying what a child one year old should be like; he is not in any danger whatever of coming into conflict with the laws of the land and being punished for it. All he is in danger of is running into the certainties or rigidities of his parents, but there is plenty of danger in that for most children.

Most parents have rather unbending ideas about what a small child should be like, how he should behave, what he should and should not do, even about when he should do it and when he should not. Most parents will not admit that these are really only matters of convenience for themselves or for the local customs of the natives, and that they have no real universal validity whatever. When a child first begins to explore his environment—the world as he sees and feels it—he doesn't know any rules. He has no taboos. He reaches out in all directions to find out what it's like. He tries to ingest everything because this is the primitive method of getting acquainted, but he finds some things can be ingested to his advantage and some things cannot. He learns to accept and to reject, and his developing morality is based simply on what is pleasant and what is found to be unpleasant.

But even today, when very small children behave in various natural ways, parents disapprove violently. The form of behavior that gets almost certain disapproval lies in the sexual area. That is, a child, one or two years old, exploring his total environment, finds, amongst everything else in his reality, his own genital area, and it still happens (though I hope and believe not as frequently as it used to) that his mother has extremely rigid ideas about genital areas, and when the child is caught engaging in such exploration, the mother expresses disapproval very emphatically.

The child should be exploring his total environment at that stage, and there should be no taboos placed upon such exploration. This is generally acceptable, but apparently many mothers haven't been told about it, or, if they have, they can't quite believe it because of the way they have been brought up themselves. Very many children meet violence for the first time in their lives from their mother at this stage of their development. It is still common for mothers to slap a child's hand and to say to him, "Dirty! Dirty! If you do that, Mother won't love you any more."

This is a very damaging experience. The part of the child's physical equipment which is associated with basic intersexual relationship has been made dirty and its existence associated with loss of love rather than with the expression of love. This is very disturbing to the whole development of the child's relationship to the opposite sex.

As he grows older, the child is afraid to find out about sexual facts of life, because this would associate his mother and his father with the badness and dirtiness that have been imposed on him as belonging to sexual equipment. To the young child, of course, genital organs are not sexual at all, only excretory; but large areas of human behavior will have been spoiled by this early disapproval, by these attitudes imposed on a small child before his intelligence, his experience, and his freedom to think independently are sufficient for him to be able to defend himself against that type of misdirection.

This is just one example of how the intelligent child, then, at a very early age, is convinced of his sin. He is loaded with a burden of guilt, fear, and anxiety. Because the very small child, busily trying to find out everything about the total environment in which he is going to have to live, eager to explore, to know, to experiment, and enjoying very much all his urges, all the things he wants to do—the use of eyes, nose, ears, hands, fingers, feet, and legs—because this child does not naturally subscribe to Mother's rules (that is in terms of the time at which he should do things, the place where he should do them, or how he should do them—or if he should do them at all), because he runs into the threat "If you do this or don't do that, Mother won't love you any more," because he feels that what he is doing is perfectly natural to him, he reaches the conclusion that he is just naturally bad. And bad, of course, means unlovable. Mother said so. And because he dare not risk the loss of love, he learns very early in life that he must go about pretending that he isn't bad, but pretending that he is good, so that he will continue to be loved.

This is a very difficult position for a child to be in, because he can never act freely any more. He must watch all the time to see what he should do, what he is supposed to do. He knows what he naturally would do, but this has been called bad. He can hope only to learn from good people what they expect of him.

His mother, by definition, is "good" in the child's eyes, because she is what good is. She decides what is good and what is bad and is the primary authority on goodness and badness. Even God is only brought in to support the mother. He doesn't originate anything; the mother originates it. Two different mothers on opposite sides of the street may have quite different ideas of good and bad but God is made to support both of them, one just as firmly as the other.

The old saying that "Mother knows best" was regarded, and still is, in many places, as practically sacred. Few children have the temerity to ask how she knows, who told her, where she studied, what is her authority, whenever she says, "Mother knows best." Most children do not have that degree of freedom with their parents. They would be beaten down if they tried—not necessarily physically, but in one way or another. But Mother continues to make the rules.

Very many children, when these things happen to them, become very shy, afraid to face new circumstances, afraid to meet new people, afraid of the dark, afraid of all kinds of things; irrationally afraid, because they don't know how to cope with new circumstances at all. They have no confidence in natural behavior, because they have learned that natural behavior is bad and disapproved of by good people. In unknown circumstances or new situations the child is afraid to act at all for fear he will be "found out" as bad and be discarded, unloved, and unaccepted.

Thus the groundwork is laid, to a certain extent, for the beginning of the well-known inferiority complex, which those of us who have become civilized forcibly in childhood must inevitably suffer from to one degree or another. The degree will depend on the amount of fear used to train us and on how early we were beaten into conformity with the local customs of the natives, as understood by our parents.

Of course no parents deliberately do these things to their children. They do not coolly decide to hurt their children. They do not set out to impose an inferiority complex on a defenseless child. They are merely following the way they themselves were brought up, and they believe that this is the good way because it was imposed on them in childhood.

But it cannot be overemphasized that basic security comes from being loved—or more importantly—from feeling loved when one is very small. There is nothing new in this concept. Indeed, implied in all the world's great religions there has been the suggestion or the command that people should love each other, should "Love thy neighbor as thyself." The catch, of course, comes in the last bit, "as thyself." Most of us who were brought up to be moral children, good children, a credit to our parents (according to the local customs of the natives) before we were four or five or six years old, are incapable of loving ourselves, because we were convinced in early childhood that we were not naturally lovable. We could only appear to be lovable by pretending to be something other than we were. And if we cannot love ourselves in a healthy way, then it is not possible for us to really love anyone else, because we project our own hatred of ourselves on other people.

We have been talking about what not to do to children—how not to bind them to the "certainties" of the past, how not to deceive them with so-called harmless lies, how not to stunt their emotional development with the cruelest threat of all—that of the loss of love. But our responsibilities lie much deeper than a negative or even a passive level. There are certain positive things that we can and must do for our children; there are certain positive things that we can and must teach them.

Our children need to learn, early in life, values that go away beyond the advantage of the group, the father, the mother, the family, and the local natives. They can be introduced and should be introduced to world values long before they go to school, and children are capable of recognizing the existence and importance of such values if their parents show that knowledge and that feeling themselves.

We do know what teachers need in children who come to school for the first time, that is, well-educated and intelligent teachers, who are free to think for themselves. They want children who have some points of view, some knowledges, freedoms to think, children who are not nailed to the mast of an absolute belief, but who are capable of considering all peoples' attitudes and of finding what is useful in them and discarding what is not, on the initiative of their own intelligence and not because some of their ancestors said or wrote this or that, even if it was written down in a Constitution. Children need a sense of identity with the whole human race.

These are the kinds of children that are needed when they come to school. The responsibility is overwhelmingly that of the parents, who should be able to introduce their children to certain facts, to orient them reasonably effectively in relation to time, so that they do not think and feel only in the present but feel themselves part of the long processes of development, not just local time, not just since the birth of "myself" or "my father" or "my grandfather," but national time, human racial time, geological time, astronomical time. These concepts are well within the scope of a small child before he goes to school; not in detail, not in measurements or anything like that, but in knowledge that these things exist and are a part of human experience, and are the context in which man is or is not going to survive. Particularly schools need children who are already reaching forward into time, ahead of themselves.

If parents spend all their money on payments for things they can't afford, so that they never have any money, and are always being pressed or pushed and just living for the moment, their children are not going to get proper appreciation of future time. A child by the time he goes to school should, if his parents present an example, be able to save up whatever he needs for at least a week or a month ahead to get something more valuable than he could get with what he has now.

Nowadays and in our present culture, by the time a boy or girl is in his early twenties or even his middle teens, he needs to be able to function about ten years ahead so that he will be able to project ahead of himself a picture of the kind of person he proposes to be after ten years or so of education and training. Otherwise he will not plan his life; he will continue to be the creature of accident in this field as well as in many other fields.

In other areas as well, such as his relation to place, a child should have learned by the time he goes to school to feel at home anywhere in space. Of course I do not mean this literally, but he should know of the existence of space and be aware of his relationship to it.

This task is much easier since the comic strips and television have "gone for" the space concept. To be sure it is somewhat distorted, but it's much better than not having any idea at all. It is very much better than the concept that many children used to get from their parents that there wasn't any place that mattered outside of the local community. It is rare to find a benefit from the comics, but this, I think, is one—that children are escaping from their locality. It may be into fantasy, but still it is an enlargement of experience beyond local boundaries.

In relation to things, children have a great deal of developing to do. When they are born, their relation to things is entirely ingestive. It is just that they want to absorb anything that can be absorbed, as an amoeba does, in the most primitive way of coping with things. A lot of people continue to be amoebas all their lives, trying to get hold of and incorporate anything they can; just to have stuff and things is regarded as of itself creditable and productive of a feeling of superiority. A child should be able to be relatively independent of things by the time he goes to school. At least, he should be able to discriminate between things which are just temporarily amusing and those which are really permanently valuable. Again this is a responsibility of his parents.

A child's relationship with persons is of such generally recognized importance that it needs no lengthy discussion here. We are all aware that a child's relationship to persons all through his life will be very largely determined during the first weeks and months of his life by his relationship with his mother or the substitute for his mother.

The greatest service that parents can give their children is to help them to reach reality, reality as it is known at the present time, and to give them the freedom to change this reality, to change their attitudes as more knowledge becomes available, to adjust to changed circumstances without guilt, without feelings of sin, without anxiety, and without being afraid to think naturally or to accept their own naturalness. If we can give our children this, then undoubtedly they will be able to develop away beyond our level of maturity, become much more mature than we have been or can hope to be because of the handicaps of our particular upbringing.

WESTON LA BARRE

The Riddle of the Sphinx

In this contribution a distinguished anthropologist discusses the transitions from childhood love in each sex to adult forms of love. The male, especially in the Western world, has a much more difficult time making these adjustments than does the female. He is in constant contact with the mother, as is the female, but whereas the model of the mother remains continuously before the girl as the object with which to identify, the boy has eventually to reject the maternal for the paternal model. This is a switch he is required to make from the moment when, as a little child, he is told that he is a little man. It is a difficult switch to make at best, and some never achieve it; those who do not often repress any appearance of love or tenderness in themselves—first because it is associated with "the weaker sex," and second because the identification with the masculine ideal requires such a taboo on tenderness. Hence, as Professor La Barre points out, women have several ways of loving, but men have only one.

> *Man's love is of man's life is a thing apart,*
> *'Tis woman's whole existence.*

La Barre discusses in this article such questions as how women become polymorphously loving, how they come to love men, and whether or not their love of men is any different from the love which men have for women.

Everyone knows the Riddle that the Sphinx asked Oedipus as he traveled along a road alone. "What is it that walks on four legs, then on two legs, and then on three?" Many men, say the Greeks, lost their lives in not being able to answer it. But all of us now know the answer. It is man. As a baby he creeps on all fours; when he learns to walk, he stands erect; and when he is old, he walks with a cane. But the Riddle and its answer are deceptively simple. When studied and thought

"The Riddle of the Sphinx" (editor's title). From Weston La Barre, *The Human Animal* (Chicago: The University of Chicago Press, 1954), pp. 208–18. Copyright © 1954 by The University of Chicago Press.

about, the meaning becomes deeper and deeper. For man is also the mammal whose inner essence lies in his extraordinary ability to love others of his own kind, varyingly with age and circumstance.

The fact is complicated, too, since man has a number of ways of loving, several of which he must learn in order to become human. As a child he must love in one way, but as an adult in others. Thus the Riddle that the Sphinx puts to the animal that lives in families is much more complex. Each individual is asked it at some point on his road through life. And if he cannot answer it, he dies, in so far as his full potential as a man is concerned. In this form the Riddle is more baffling: "Who may love, but not love the one whom he loves?" The answer is the same: man. It was in solving this Riddle that man finally became human. And it is in resolving it that each individual person finally reaches his own moral "gerontomorphic" manhood.

Anatomically, man's humanity does consist in this vertical two-legged posture that the Greek answer implies. Physiologically, his humanity rests on an exaggeration of mammalian traits, and not on their organic repression or evolutionary loss. Psychologically, it is just this exaggeration of both dependency and sexuality that brings such grave problems of inter-individual adjustment of behavior within the human family. This is no problem for the wild animal. There is no conflict between the two aspects of its mammalian behavior. For in wild animals, breeding and maternal care operate in alternation and do not occur within the same span of time. That is, the sexuality of wild animals is ordinarily seasonal. The sexes breed and separate; the offspring are born when the female is alone; and the dependency of the young is over in a season. The female's roles as protective mother and as breeding mate do not occur during the same time period; for when the next breeding season comes around, the young usually have departed. And if, later, adult son breed with mother, he may do so on the same competitive terms as any other male.

This never happens in any human society. For the universal human family is a semi-permanent living-together of both adults and young. Indeed, the bodily adaptations to the family manner of life are physically evident, as we have seen, in the actual bodies of men, women, and children. Their very sexual dimorphism and racial differences grow out of it. In humans the adult male is specialized in strength and aggression and potency for the purposes of the permanent family group, as permanent mate and as protector and as father—just as the human female has specializations of general mammalian behavior which also contribute their part, and just as the infantilizations of the human baby are at the root of several aspects of our humanity. Man uses the family in the service of his heightened instinctual needs. But the family also uses him, converting both his strength and his potency to its service—in time, perhaps, even triumphing a little over his individual anthropoid cantankerousness. Family life achieves the final domestication of the male too.

But it is a genital and not a philoprogenitive drive that does it. The human male has no instincts, no anatomy, and no physiology to teach him to love the child as such. If the male learn the pleasures of paternity as opposed to those of procreation, it is the result of the mother's teaching him, and through some identification of his with mother and child—and not because as a mere male he knew all about it beforehand, or got some organic satisfaction out of the little beast. Furthermore, the selfish, opinionated, irascible featherless biped that man is, would not by inveterate and universal habit live in mixed sexual and age aggregates—the ambiguous blessings of his bachelor freedom a memory of the past—were it not that, on the whole, he found it more fun to do so than otherwise. Males form sexual associations with females not out of a tiresome, dutiful, pious, half-unwilling obedience to the demands of the culture but in fulfilment of the biological nature of the beast. The family is not a creation of culture: without the family there would be no culture!

In thinking of the long human latency period in his last extended work, Freud asked a significant anthropological question:

> [Consider] the hypothesis that man is descended from a mammal which reached sexual maturity at the age of five, but that some great external influence was brought to bear upon the species and interrupted the straight line of sexuality. This may also have been related to some other transformation in the sexual life of man as compared with that of animals.

Since all the anthropoids other than man reach a relatively early sexual maturity, this is a reasonable conjecture. On good primate and anthropoid evidence, we believe that this "external influence" upon latency was the increasingly familial association of hominids. For an increased dependency and slower growth in the infant are concurrent with the growth of the permanent non-seasonal sexuality of the adult and the increasing cohesion of the family. Indeed, we have seen that this infantilization of the child, in the long delay of sexual maturity, is related to the human "fetalization of the ape" and to those "infantilizations" or evolutionary fixations which constitute racial traits. Furthermore, the "transformation of the sexual life of man" certainly includes the setting-up of the universal human incest-taboo, as also does "familial symbiosis" in man and the manifold physical manifestations this has wrought. The change from seasonal estrus or "heat" to the year-round operation of the menstrual cycle in the female and the permanent sexual drive of the male are also clear "transformations in the sexual life of man" and his anthropoid relatives.

From a heightening of mammalian functions, both of dependency and of sexuality, the new symbiotic unit, the human family, necessarily posed problems. Of course other problems had to have been previously solved biologically, for new solutions to be built on this base. Indeed, the organs of the mother-child relationship, and the organs of male-female relationship and their heightened physiology, are peculiarly evident in the human animal. These are no problem. The problem arises with respect to the living-together of other members of the family.

For the anatomy of paternal love is missing, as it is also missing between males in general. In fact, the male in the old-style mammal was largely structured for aggressive competition with other males of its own species, as well as for fighting its natural wild enemies of other species. But if others than mere heterosexual mates are to live together in the human family—and if still larger social aggregates are to be formed—then some new adaptive mechanism is necessary among humans.

This adaptive mechanism is culture. Culture is the non-bodily and non-genetic contriving of bonds of agreement that enable this animal to function as human. Such relationships—of father and son, and of male and male—must be forged *morally*. They can operate only through the discipline of aggression, through identification with one another, through the contriving of communication and understandings, and through the discovery or invention of agreements and compromises. Women often wonder that men are so passionately concerned with generalizations and with principles, when from a female point of view all human relations seem so simple and uncomplex, being given in her anatomy. But the simple fact is, that males do not have female bodies: human males need principles and agreements by very virtue of their being males and being the kind of animal that necessarily and still usefully embodies the old mammalian male aggressiveness. No amount of feminine example and persuasion can un-teach the honest masculine animal of this knowledge of his nature.

Moral bonds and cultural structures—styles of thinking—are an area of men's present and future evolution that are not yet and probably never will be made bodily organs and somatized. It may be true that some of the arts—probably pottery, agriculture, and weaving —are the inventions of women. But principle or generalization is a male artifact: the *logos* that is the endless preoccupation of male metaphysics. What connects father and son, male and male, is the mystery of *logos* and logos alone: logos as the literal "word" which conveys linguistic meaning and understanding; logos as laws, agreements, rules, and regularities of behavior; logos as the implicit means and substance of common understanding and communication, and of cultural joining in the same styles of thinking; and logos as shared pattern, within which father can identify with son and permit his infancy, within which son can identify with father and become a man, and within which a male can perceive and forgive the equal manhood of his fellow-man. This does not mean, of course, that women are biologically unable to become great philosophers, creators of literature, or indeed scientists—all of whom are concerned with generalization— but it does mean, as is historically manifest, that men are more characteristically and inescapably motivated to formulate principles and generalizations. For, biologically, women are closer to realistic particulars.

Primitive men know rightly that women can make children with their bodies. But it takes men to make men, that is, members of the tribe. Hence that universal preoccupation among men everywhere with initiation, that mysterious male re-birth of the youth into full membership in the society of men. Often in this the initiates are actually taught the tribal lore formally and the metaphysical "facts of life," forcibly and fearfully indoctrinated in the supernatural wisdom that holds the male group together. Often, as with the Arunta and their tribal lore of the *churinga* or bull-roarer, the cultural nature of this wisdom is pitifully evident. Often, as with the Zuñi, when the youth learns that the masked gods who have whipped him are only men of the tribe and that he must now wear the god-mask himself, the nature of man's cultural burden becomes poignantly evident. But no matter: these myths serve. The initiates may also be tested in the enduring of pain; and sometimes they are painfully marked with the male sign of tribal membership. (A woman can give proof of her femaleness in a very simple and irrefutable way, by having a baby—but a male must always *prove* something, his manhood within the group. What reason, indeed, would press women to create great poetry, music, or art—when they can do better than that and make real human beings!) Thus, very often the initiates must keep the secret of these male myths and mysteries from women and children, under pain of death. Perhaps primitive men are right: women don't understand these things.

The complexly mammalian human family has its characteristic rivalries and aggressions and satisfactions with each stage of physical growth and physiological maturity. There is a proper and necessary role with each stage of psychosexual development in its members, given their differential strengths and special needs. The family—with its necessary disciplines, segmental sharings, and culture-historically elaborated roles—is the font of all morality, law, and indeed of all human culture. Manifestly, seals do not have sin because they do not have human social organization biologically. Bees do not have culture because their bodies build something else, the meta-organism of the hive. The kangaroo-rat *Dipodomys* lacks morality because it lacks the biological dilemmas demanding morality. Culture is man's adaptation to his humanity. Man secretes mores partly because his humanity would otherwise not operate from friction, or would otherwise fall apart from centrifugal governorlessness, and partly because he could not otherwise survive as an animal species.

It is an error to attack Freud, who observed man's psychological predicament in the family, by thinking that he "reduced everything to sex." For this is not true. Freud was in fact pointing out that there are *other kinds* of pleasure and love than the genital. For if love is realistically defined as a tender concern for the source of one's organic pleasure, then it obviously applies to the love of a mother for her child and to a child's love for its mother, as well as to the love of a man and woman. It is of course oedipal guilt, clinging to the dependent love of the mother, which leads adults to this stubborn psychic blindness. Children know better. For they love, and they love passionately and overwhelmingly, long before genitality.

There can be no doubt that the baby does love in a dependent infantile fashion the woman who mothers him well. It is only when sexual love supervenes that the categorical imperative—the human incest-taboo—emerges. There is no mystery at all in why men love women or in why women love themselves: as children they loved their mothers. The only psychological problem is how women come to love men. A man's love for females in general may explain his affection for his daughter; but this still leaves physiologically unexplained a daughter's love for her father and her emergent love for other men. Perhaps men should enjoy this double largesse of wifely and daughterly love, and cease pondering its theoretical improbability. But in any case, as far as a man is concerned, the mature sexual love of women is permitted only if the woman so loved is not the woman *first* loved in dependent infantile fashion. This is the universal incest-taboo in all human beings wherever they are found.

The profound and provocative nature of the Riddle of the Sphinx then becomes clearer. "Who may love, but not love the one whom he loves?" The answer is human beings: of whatever kind and condition, primitive or civilized, male or female, old or young. For the Riddle admits of various solutions, at least one of which is appropriate for each human situation, and some others of which are inappropriate, because they misidentify the love object or use a non-adaptive way of loving it. For the child the solution is this: "He may love (dependently), but not love (sexually) the one whom he loves (mother)." For the adult man there is a different solution: "He may love (women, sexually), but not love (sexually) the one whom he loves (dependently once, mother)." A man has the pride and privilege, with his maleness, of returning to a woman a shared pleasure, like but unlike that which another woman, with her breast, conferred upon him first as a baby. Cherished and nurtured to strength by his mother, he may then protect and cherish another woman in his turn. And of all the things in this world these two, maternal and conjugal love, are without any qualification wholly good.

All this is a process of growth, psychological and physical, and of phatic communication culturally. It is no easy, automatic process. For the male change of phase enjoins upon him that he change almost entirely from dependent to protective love of women; for the residues of his infantile self, when in excess, are disruptive of his adult male responsibility and power to create and to provide security, and not (as once) primarily to consume it. More than that, and purely for himself, any unconscious confusion of mate with mother tends to disfranchise him of enjoyment, because of the anxiety in violating incest-taboos. Women, because they must learn to change the sex of the early love object in loving men instead of mothers, may have a difficult time adjusting to the complexities of their femininity. But men, because of this reversal of dependency roles vis-à-vis women, perhaps have the harder time growing up. Conversely, men may have less problem being male and taking their maleness for granted, in their naïve and unchanging love of women. But women, perhaps, in dependency terms, are not so fiercely and desperately embattled in growing up as men are.

For the adult woman, the answer to the Riddle is still different: "She may love (men, both sexually and dependently), but not love the one

whom she loves (neither mother, dependently, nor father, sexually)."
Thus feminine psychology is more complex. Men have to change from
the original love object, and from the child's way of loving her. But
women, in addition, have to change the sex of the original love object
in order to love men. Furthermore, adult women have several ways of
loving, but men only one. To her child the woman must now give
dependency-sustaining love, as her mother did to her, this maternal
love being of her body which is adapted to the needs of the deeply
infantilized human baby. But meanwhile, for the purposes of her
maternity, she must often give up her own competence and security in
dealing directly with the world, and accept the difficult role of a
trusting and fairly complete dependence on another person, her wisely
chosen husband. Small wonder that women in general are more
psychological-minded than men, and more skilled in reading the
minimal phatic indices of character or of emotional climate. They have
to be, biologically.

What remains puzzling psychologically is how the woman, who as a
child also first loved her mother, can make the mysterious change in
the sex of her love object and come to love her father, and hence to be
able later to love men. Some students of the problem suggest that
women depend emotionally on men to a greater degree than adult men
do on one another, and hence love dependently first the mother, then
the father, and then the husband, with the accent on the dependency.
Others believe that on the girl's identification with her mother, this
love for the mother reappears as the greater "feminine narcissism,"
which is later large enough to encompass both herself and her child
(which is herself) in mature maternal love. This explanation suggests
that the woman loves the man because he alone can give her the baby
that fulfils her femininity, as she understood femininity in childhood
through her mother. These explanations are ingenious, if labored. But
something of the mystery remains, because some women seem just
arbitrarily to love men, and we can't understand why this should be so
in terms of early childhood. Perhaps there is a touch of all-encompass-
ing maternal love in all the love that women feel, whether for children
or for men. We do not know. But we do strongly agree with our
fellow-anthropologist Ashley Montagu, that women are biologically
structured to know more about love than men do.

What we must not forget throughout is that the *psychological* sexual
constitution of the human individual is not given at birth or soon
thereafter. The human baby has no "instinctive" sexuality whatever.
True, it has primary sexual characteristics even some time before birth.

And it acquires secondary sexual characteristics at a much later puberty. But its "tertiary" sexual characteristics of psychological masculinity and femininity are quite wholly the learned experience of living in one or the other sex-defined kinds of body, and in any one of an infinity of family constellations shaped by the sexual constitutions of parental individuals. Masculinity and femininity are even shaped as roles by the expectancies of a given culture. This influence however—though Margaret Mead makes a strong case for it—is one we believe to be relatively minor, as compared with the more fundamental experience of living in a body of one specific human sex.

The fact that human sexual roles are partly learned means that human individuals, unlike wild animals, can sometimes learn wrong answers to the Riddle of the Sphinx. For example, the homosexual woman appears to have resolved the Riddle wrongly as: "She may love (women), but not love the one (father) whom she loves (and hence she cannot love men)." Or she may continue, as initially, to love women: "She may love (women sexually) but not love (dependently) the one whom she loves (mother)." For some males too, because of the child's inordinate fear of the father's categorical imperative, there come other biologically wrong answers to the Riddle. This may be either because the boy remains fixed in an outmoded dependency relationship with his dominating or over-protective mother and does not dare the rewards of a more dangerous manhood; or it may be because the permitted dependent love of the child for his mother becomes contaminated with sexualized love, and then the terror of the father forces the son to repress all love of women and to masquerade instead as a lover of men, whom he really destructively hates. The homosexual man believes that "He may love (men, in a variety of non-adaptive ways), but not love the one (mother) whom he loves (dependently and/or sexually)." He has, however, mistaken a mere object-taboo of a single specific person, his mother, for a generalized aim-taboo of a whole sex, i.e., the heterosexual love of women—which is a grievous denotative confusion. And he has also been confused about the modes and the means of love—which is a grievous connotative confusion, both symbolically and psychiatrically.

The perverse and the neurotic, therefore, contrive behavior that is in a sense "adaptive." But the behavior is adaptive not to the new biological roles of the adult in his new family-of-procreation, but adaptive rather to a childish misconception of roles, which is rooted in his old family-of-origin. For the homosexual, even in anthropoids, obviously "loves" out of fear and hatred and frustration; sporadic homosexual behavior in infra-primate animals we can only view as trial-and-error learning or *faute de mieux*. By a merely pseudo-effeminizing or meretricious infantilizing of himself, the homosexual also defrauds and unmans or effeminizes the other male. An examination of the various perverse methods of loving establishes this point clearly. The illogic of his answers to the Riddle is quite plain.

Now the biologist is quite prepared to accept any kind of organic behavior, however bizarre—if it is adaptive. For example, in *Ceratias holboelli*, a curious deep-sea fish in which it is difficult for the sexes to find each other, there is a vascular connection between the female and the parasitic male, the latter receiving bountiful nourishment for further growth and maturity—in order to fertilize the female. This extraordinary behavior is obviously adaptive biologically. But neurotic behavior is "adaptive" only psychologically, and adaptive only to a misconceived view of biological roles. For it is difficult to see how a "love" based on fear, destructive hatred, and frustration of one's own and others' essential biological nature can be adaptive. To rob someone of his or her love of the other sex, and hence to rob them also of paternity or maternity, is doubly to rob the individual of his full human potentiality. The biologist is therefore forced to conclude that behavior which is non-adaptive biologically, but only adaptive psychologically, is properly not his concern but the psychiatrist's; that homosexuality among humans is not a genuine variety of love but a dishonest and desperate neurotic game, arising from tragic unsuccess in escaping from the family-of-origin to a family-of-procreation. Neither biologist nor psychiatrist can accept the views of literary apologists from Plato to Gide that homosexuality is a "normal" abnormality. For the normal process is clear. A girl becomes a woman by an identification with her mother and through a mysterious change in the sex of her original love object. A boy must become a man by similarly admiring manliness—in a rival he may hate or envy—through the mysterious love of male *logos,* not of physical males. When he begins to discover this logos or pattern in himself, he gives up wishing to destroy the father, but instead identifies with him and wishes to become like the father, in admiration of things masculine that comes out later as a normal adult manly self-confidence.

The psychiatrists, no doubt rightly, tell us that there is no neurosis without some basic libidinal role-misidentification. In this lies the value of their explanations of psychopathy for a biologically oriented understanding of the human animal. Their findings also fit in exactly with those of the physical anthropologist. For the family is the factory of human sexuality. The process is very largely one of individual life-history, post-natal, and conditioned. Psychologists agree that man's very sexuality is not furnished with instinctive channelings. It is, in fact, the dependent human child's very lability, ductility, and eductability which make the socialization process possible. Man does not have completely structured sexual instincts which fit him soon to adult animal life. The only "instincts" he is born with, such as the grasping and the sucking reflexes, are minimally and specifically those that fit him to the condition of the human infant. And the cultural anthropologist agrees with them all: for he is aware that man either invents his own responses, or accepts those invented for him.

Man has "socialization." His significant speciation is not the racial, but his post-natal, moral, and superorganic *learning*. So far from being born full-panoplied with instincts adjusting it to an adult solitary state, the human child on the contrary is born in a very markedly plastic, neurologically immature, "neurobiotactical," and educable socializable state. His moral humanity is not a hereditary given, but an artifact of social stimuli. For the child is biologically dependent upon his parents, *vulnerable* to the social influences of adults, and hence a potential culture-bearer. This basic inter-individuality is biologically given in the nature of his species. But what is done with it, and through it, varies from society to society and from family to family. The child is the domesticate of the man.

"Human nature," therefore, in this sense is not automatically organic, not instinctually spontaneous, but necessarily disciplined and shaped by a long apprenticeship to childhood. A child perforce becomes a Right Thinker before he learns to think at all. His very language is an arbitrary given, which teaches him the canons wherewith he must apperceive reality; and it is doubtful whether, after this seduction, he can ever again peer around the veil of language and gaze on naked nature with pristine innocence. His language is at once an aspect of his culture and the major vehicle of his socialization to all the rest of the culture. Indeed, by looking at the human child and its predicaments, it is very easy to see how mere relative cultural fiats become emotional absolutes. It is clear enough how moral commands, introjected or taken in from hard necessity, seem in turn logically necessary and "hard" when re-projected again as institutions, value systems, religions, and cultures. He has been "taken in," so to speak, by what he has taken in.

PERCIVAL M. SYMONDS

Love and Self-Love

This contribution represents the second half of Professor Symonds' chapter on "Love and Self-Love" reprinted from his splendid book The Dynamics of Human Adjustment. *In the first half of the chapter the author shows how love develops in the interactive relationship between mother and child. In the second half he discusses the ways in which love may be displaced from parents to other persons, and the kinds of choices made by males and females in their selection of love objects.*

Symonds also considers a common phenomenon in our civilization—namely, the rejection of love—and analyzes its causes. Love is so little understood in the Western world that it appears paradoxical to state that hostility is usually an evidence, a signal, of the need for love; that hostility is, in fact, love—frustrated. That love is the strongest of all civilizing factors is a point which requires endless repetition to become part of the practical conduct of human beings the world over, and loving kindness should be a part of any learning situation, as Professor Symonds stresses.

Finally, Symonds discusses the importance of self-acceptance and self-love in the search for a stable, healthy life.

Displacement of Love

MOTIVATION   It has been mentioned earlier that love is first given by a child to his parents and then later is directed toward other persons and objects. This takes place by a process of displacement—of shifting attitudes and feelings from one person to another. There are several reasons why a child does not find his first love toward his parents entirely satisfactory and does not maintain it as the exclusive relationship throughout childhood and later life. By spreading his love among a number of persons, he reduces the danger of frustration and failure. To pin all one's hopes on one person is like putting all one's

"Love and Self-Love." From Percival M. Symonds, *The Dynamics of Human Adjustment* (New York: D. Appleton-Century Co., 1946), pp. 554–65. Copyright © 1946, renewed 1974. Reprinted by permission of Prentice-Hall, Inc., Englewood Cliffs, N.J.

eggs in one basket. To have many friends rather than one and to be able to go to other persons for relief and consolation is safer than relying on one person. This is particularly true because of the child's hostile feelings toward his parents and his fear of retaliation from them. If there is a possibility that through his hostile feelings he may lose them, it may be safe to turn some of his love to grandfather or grandmother, brother or sister, or companions outside of the home. So spreading one's love to other persons affords relief from the painful dependence on the mother, painful because of the possibility that it is not permanent and that the child may suffer disappointment.

As one shifts his love from one person to another, he lessens his burden of conflict and guilt. Confining his love to one person, he has to suffer the possible effect of his hostile tendencies. There is safety in spreading one's affections among many people.

Still another aspect in the motivation of the displacement of love is that by finding value in another person, one re-creates in fantasy the earlier person, perhaps the mother, who had been destroyed in fantasy. So throughout life there follows a succession of attachments in which the new person takes the place of someone who occupied a similar position in the past.

Sometimes displacement of love occurs because the original love does not satisfy. The mother who is disappointed in what she expected to receive in her marriage from her husband may give herself passionately and devotedly to her children. They become the recipients of her affection that is not reciprocated by her husband. Writers commonly make it seem as though the responsibility for this failure lay with the husband, who is pictured as a remote and unresponsive person immersed in his professional or business interests. But the basis for the displacement lies equally with the narcissistic mother who finds it difficult to give herself wholeheartedly to her mate. As another illustration, a child who loses one parent frequently lavishes too much love on the parent who is left, in fear lest he lose this parent too. This concentration of love may become so powerful that hostile impulses naturally present may be stifled and repressed. Repressed hostility is always a dangerous condition and leads to profound changes of character and possibly neurotic (hysterical) manifestations.

BASIS FOR THE DISPLACEMENT OF LOVE   In any case of infatuation or attraction there is some element bridging the gap between the new loved object and a person who has been loved in the past. This element may be some isolated characteristic of the person, subtle and tenuous, such as the timbre of the voice, a gesture, a shrug, a fleeting odor. Elusive as such an element may be, it is still real and exerts the all-controlling influence in determining the strength of the new attraction based on pleasant associations with the past.

DISPLACEMENT OF LOVE VARIES IN COMPLETENESS AND PERMA-NENCE   The displacement of love varies in its completeness and permanence. Some relationships represent a broad and deep experience, while others are shallow and superficial. The personality dynamics of the individual determines whether he has a need that is to be temporary or permanent. The quality of a new relationship also depends on the strength of the needs of the two individuals concerned. If the relationship fulfils profound ego needs, if there is deep satisfaction in the reparation to which the relationship gives expression, then the relationship may be more stable than if it satisfies more isolated and immediate needs in the individual. In general it may be stated that the stability of the love relationship depends on the degree to which it satisfies embracing, inclusive needs rather than isolated needs of the individual.

It is difficult for one love object to correspond to all of the requirements of the imago. Adolescence is a time when many temporary crushes and alliances spring into being, each one of which corresponds to some inner need within the individual, but none of which satisfies all needs equally well. The tendency to have a succession of temporary and superficial love relationships is known as "Don Juanism," after a legendary Spanish figure who traditionally was an irresistible lover and seducer of many women. Popularly the Don Juan is thought of as being a particularly ardent and passionate person. Actually the man who flits from one love-affair to another is amatorially weak. He frequently is less concerned with his passion than with his hostility. He may be so haunted by the fear of death to his loved ones as the result of his hostile impulses toward them that as a form of insurance he provides himself with a succession of love objects. He may have to prove his own virility and irresistibleness by his repeated courtships. He also may have to assure himself that his love object is not indispensable because if he loses one, he will never be without another to take her place. The Don Juan then is haunted by his fears of being left alone, of his own possible lack of virility and passion, and of the destructive effects of his hostilities.

It is a tradition that a man is inclined to change his love objects more frequently than a woman. A woman is supposed to find special need for the permanence of the love relationship, partly because she is economically dependent on the man, since it is she who bears a child and must have permanence in order to rear it properly. A man does not feel the urgency of this responsibility, at least in the same degree. Constancy in love in a man depends on many factors, the most important of which is the degree to which he has been accepted as a child and finds values in the permanence and stability of his own childhood family relationships. This is aided, in addition, by the man's identification with his mother, which helps him to understand the woman's need and tendency to preserve what she loves. In this we are saying that constancy in a man depends in part on the strength of the feminine component in his nature. This identification also helps to the extent that his wish to have his own mother as his child (a very important and common infantile fantasy) becomes realized in his ability to play this mother rôle toward his wife.

It has been pointed out that displacement, at least from the mother to other loved objects, should not be too complete. It is desirable for satisfactory later love experiences that traces of the love for the parents should remain. The person who forgets his earlier loves too completely may forget how to love at all. Except as one can displace into the new situation the traces of the old, it is possible that love in the new situation will never satisfactorily develop. While too strong fixation of love handicaps because it can inhibit the formation of new love relationships, on the other hand, a tender feeling which is the remnant of an earlier more ardent feeling should persist throughout life as a sign of the individual's love capacity.

Persons Toward Whom Love May Be Directed

PARENTS AND SIBLINGS   Enough has been said to make clear that love is first directed toward one's parents. For both boys and girls the mother is the most important first person because from her come milk and the accompanying tenderness. But the father, from whom one receives support and firmness, follows closely in importance. This love spreads to other members of the family, particularly to siblings. Indeed, sibling relationships help to lessen the intensity, with its accompanying dangers, of love for the parents. The development of sibling love also helps to hamper tendencies toward jealousy, rivalry, and hate of the siblings. Love may also spread to the grandparents, who not infrequently stand as superparental figures to be worshiped with awe, if not loved in a more immediate and direct way. By displacement, love may be felt toward one's in-laws and also, in the case of foster children, toward foster parents.

NEW FAMILY TIES   Part of the process of achieving adulthood is the establishment of new marital and family relationships. As children are added to the family group, each is given a due measure of love and affection. Attitudes of love toward one's children are usually displacements of earlier loves felt toward father or mother or brothers or sisters in childhood. A mother may love each of her children in a different way, each representing a displacement of her attitudes toward one or another member of her own family in childhood and infancy or even toward the different imagos of any one family member. The typical stages of displacement of love are from parents to siblings and later for the boy to other boy friends, then to an older woman, and finally to a girl of his own age, with eventual consummation in the marriage relationship.

DISPLACEMENTS OF LOVE OUTSIDE THE FAMILY   These displacements of love are not confined to the family circle. Less intense but equally important are the many friendships which represent milder forms of love attachment. Friendships may be crystallized in group allegiances as a man joins a club, a society, an athletic team, or political party.

It is not uncommon for love to be turned toward animals. A man can become as fond of his horse or dog as of a friend and will mourn its loss as though it were someone near and dear to him. The animal cemetery in Hartsdale, New York, with its elaborate stone monuments erected to household pets, is testimony to the strength of these love attachments turned toward animals.

One may also love inanimate objects and less tangible things such as enterprises, causes, ideas, and so on. One may devote considerable allegiance to a business enterprise or an athletic contest, and throw into such activities some of the zeal which might, on another occasion, characterize a love relationship with an individual. One may devote a considerable amount of love to things such as possessions, money, clothing, and collections of various kinds. The curator of the museum, the capitalist, the director of the botanical garden devote their interests and passion to the care and preservation of these enterprises as truly as the mother does to her growing child. When an object also acquires the power for sexual stimulation, it is known as a fetish. Objects furnish such stimulation when they have special symbolic value and permit the repetition of pleasurable situations that occurred in a simpler setting in early infancy. A shoe, a glove, a ribbon, or a handkerchief may be a symbol of the absent loved person and originally, perhaps, will serve as a substitute for the absent mother. The philosopher or scientist is in love with his thoughts and ideas, cherishes the words which he places on paper, and becomes angry with his publisher who may insist that less important passages be deleted or awkwardly phrased statements reworded.

Enough has been said already to indicate that one important direction that love may take is toward the self. Someone has described sleep as a withdrawal of interests from the outside world and the concentration of them on the self. It is well known that dreams are wholly egocentric, and regardless of their apparent subject-matter, they always have direct personal reference.

Selection of the Love Object

NARCISSISTIC LOVE CHOICE This has two features: the selection of someone who will give the person praise and support; and the selection of someone who will be like himself. With regard to the first, which Freud has called "anaclitic love choice," one selects as a person to be loved someone who will fill the place of father and mother. The love object is selected as someone who will love him in return, who will protect, sustain, and support him, who will praise him for his deeds and accomplishments. Even in the most mature love relationship there is always a trace of this factor in the selection.

The other phase of the narcissistic love choice is the selection of a person who in some way is like the self. Freud has said that the person selected may represent one's present qualities, whether of appearance, intellect, or personality; one's childhood qualities; one's ideals and aspirations; or, in the case of one's own child, he may once have been an actual part of the self.

Every object-love relationship is based in part on narcissistic love. If one finds that the other person represents a fulfilment of his own deeper longings and aspirations, that person may appear attractive and valuable; and this is the basis of mature love. Those who have made studies of marriage relationships describe a phenomenon known as "assortative mating," by which is meant that these two individuals are more like each other in various aspects than if the selection were purely random. It is well known that a man usually chooses a girl of the same nationality, race, and religion. He also usually selects her from his same economic and social class. Commonly there is some adherence to the same customs. Less known but equally true is the fact that there tends to be a resemblance in physical and intellectual measurements.

OBJECT-LOVE CHOICE   While every object-love choice has a narcissistic element in it, in the more mature forms of love other factors also play a part. Where childhood relationships in the family have been wholesome and were not accompanied by too much anxiety or repression, a person tends to select as a lover someone having the same characteristics as the father or mother. However, when guilt becomes too strong the love selection cannot be based on such obvious similarities; frequently there is a reaction formation, and the loved person bears precisely the opposite characteristics to father or mother. A man, for instance, may pick out a brunette, whereas his mother may have blonde characteristics. Or the girl whose father is a successful banker or industrial leader may choose a husband who is a writer or scientist. In these illustrations the displacement is from the parent of the opposite sex. A woman may select as a mate a man who in some way resembles her younger brother so that she can continue to play the same maternal rôle toward her husband that she played toward her brother as a child. Or in similar fashion, a man may select for a wife a girl who resembles his sister in some remote fashion, so that he may continue to play the big brother rôle toward her. However, the origin of this displacement is not limited to members of one's childhood family, but may extend to anyone with whom one has had close, tender, erotic, or libidinal relationships. A childhood nurse, a distant relative, or a family friend who has stimulated the child in some way may serve as a model for a later love choice. In every encounter with another person there is an unconscious evaluation of his characteristics, and a response is made to some characteristic associated with another person in the past who originally elicited the same special feeling.

Overvaluation of Love and Sex

BY MEN   While love tends in our present civilization to be overvalued and sex to be undervalued, in certain individuals this is not true. Some men, for instance, tend to place too strong a value on sex. To them sex is the most exciting and important thing in the world; everything is measured in terms of its contribution to sex needs. A man may overvalue sex as a way of meeting certain anxieties and of contributing in a neurotic way to the satisfaction of other needs. First of all there is the fear many men have of not being normal, particularly of not being sexually virile. This probably is a final repository of earlier anxieties which have settled on a concern over sexual adequacy. One may suspect that the man who overvalues sex is struggling with more pervasive doubts as to his adequacy as a person. The man who overvalues sex has strong needs to surpass his male rivals. Perhaps he has had these exaggerated rivalries as a boy, and they may go back to his original rivalry with his father. The sexually ardent man is attempting to restore his wounded self-esteem. He wants to prove that he can attract women and to dispel doubts as to any weakness that he may have in this direction.

In a more specific sense, sex may be overvalued because of specific early experiences. The boy who has been sexually stimulated or seduced as an infant may be made by such experiences to have an increased need for such pleasures, particularly when he feels they are to be denied.

BY WOMEN   Women in particular are inclined to set a high premium on love experiences, and while they may also overvalue sex, the sexual aspects typically play a lesser role. The woman for whom love experiences have an exaggerated significance perhaps doubts her own love qualities. Frequently she is attempting to surpass female rivals and to prove to herself that she is more attractive and more to be desired than others in her circle. This, too, goes back to a rivalry with sisters or, in the first instance, with the mother.

Women seek love experiences for the restoration of wounded self-esteem. Love serves as a compensation for the inferior sex role they are forced to play. Since a woman does not play the aggressive sex role, she has to prove that she can attract men. Horney emphasizes the need of some women to be constantly surrounded by men and build themselves an entourage as protection against the anxieties their own feelings of inferiority arouse. Another explanation sometimes adduced for the overvaluation of love by women is the fact that they have been commonly denied other pleasures and satisfactions granted to men. In the Victorian era the compartmentalization of life allotted few other interests to women than love, whereas men had the whole range of life's interests from which to draw.

Women as well as men may have been overstimulated in early childhood, and these early experiences may have forced love and sex relations to assume a place of large importance.

A little girl, for instance, who was forced by her parents to sing and dance in a tavern and was fondled by the rough visitors may have developed a taste for sensuous experiences which afterward when repressed contributed to the development of a chronic depression arising from persistent guilt.

Repudiation of Love

MOTIVATION   *Lack of Confidence in the Self.* To go to the other extreme, it is not uncommon in the present civilization to find individuals who have forced love out of their lives, at least the love of other persons. These individuals become emotionally dried up and withered. They concentrate their energies on their work and starve themselves for the richer, more meaningful, more pleasurable, and more emotional human associations. The repudiation of love is founded on a lack of confidence in the self which owes its origin to early experiences. The person who dodges love is one who feels unworthy of love. But since few young persons can accept unworthiness in themselves, it is a common tendency to rationalize the repudiation by projecting it onto others and ascribing lovelessness to them. An individual explains that he has given up love because the world is such a friendless place and other people are so interested in themselves and their own affairs. Doubts as to one's capacity to love in one situation tend to spread. The person who suffers a disappointment in a love relationship, perhaps through no fault of his own, should beware lest his misfortune drive him to a more general withdrawal. Silas Marner became the miser that he was because of one unfortunate experience when he was falsely accused of theft.

Repudiation of Love as Method of Preserving Love. Another motive for the repudiation of love is the desire to preserve love. The one love experience may have seemed so perfect and so vivid that the danger of wrecking it by future less passionate contacts is too great to be faced. To cut off a love relationship is one way of preserving it, particularly if the person feels unworthy of so vivid a love experience.

Betty, who meets the boy from Cleveland at a dance, decides that she does not care to see him again. She likes him very much, but she is afraid that further contacts will spoil the experience. This is because she is insecure in her own relationships with her mother and doubts the depth or permanence of any relationship.[1]

Dread of Intimacy. Still another reason for the repudiation of love is dread of the intimacy which a love relation entails and fear that in an intimate relationship the other person will see through one's mask to the hollowness, shallowness, and inadequacy beneath. It is for this reason that some persons insist on maintaining superficial and distant friendships. They cannot afford to risk more intimate relationships lest they reveal themselves and all the inadequacies they feel they must keep concealed.

Love Repudiated to Reduce Danger of Frustration. Love is repudiated in order to reduce the danger of frustration. The person who finds it necessary to avoid intimate relationships is one who has been burned by them in the past. He needs to avoid the possibility of rebuffs to overtures he may make because the coldness and repulse of others is more than he can bear. These frustrating situations may go back to weaning in infancy and to other situations that bred in him distrust of the attitude of others toward him.

Love Repudiated to Avoid Dependency. Still others avoid love experiences because they are afraid of the dependency they may imply. The adolescent boy or girl apparently rejects love in his own family because he is so strenuously striving to achieve independence. He does not want to feel that he is tied down to a dependence on his sister or his mother. This again is to an extent illusory. The adolescent boy who apparently is trying to avoid love experiences may be the very one for whom they are especially important. The threat that love may be withdrawn is so great to him that he may beat the gun and be the first to repudiate his need of it. There are those who are afraid of being loved too possessively. It is of interest that possession by another person is sometimes interpreted as the equivalent of disapproval. That is, if a mother resists signs of independence in her son, she also does not really respect him as a separate personality, and in this sense is disapproving. The person who strives to absorb another person is really loving narcissistically, and most persons are only too sensitive to situations in which they are being used to satisfy the needs of another.

Presence of Ambivalent Trends. The sixth basis for the repudiation of love is the presence of strong ambivalent trends. When strong hostile tendencies are backed by unconscious death wishes, the danger of

[1] P. Blos, *The Adolescent Personality*, Case of "Betty."

doing away with the person toward whom love is felt is so strong that the person does not dare to risk giving his love. Love implies a wish to protect; and if this is in conflict with hostile impulses, then the danger from these impulses may be too great a threat for the nurturing tendencies. Many a mother has rationalized her philosophy of child-rearing on the grounds that a child can be hurt by too much coddling and pampering. Actually, however, the truth may be that unconscious hostile tendencies may be so overwhelmingly strong that the mother does not dare to show too much affection to the child lest the viper in her also sting.

Fear of Depreciation. A seventh basis for the repression of love is the fear of depreciation by others. No one wishes to place himself in a situation where he is likely to be criticized or humbled. A person may give himself to another who responds, not generously, but selfishly and without appreciation. Some persons are unable to bear such a threat.

Repression of Love through Identification. There are some who have actually been trained to repress their love tendencies. Perhaps they come from families in which the open expression of love is stifled and the family pattern is established so that only the barest tokens of affection are permitted expression. Some persons are used to showing their love awkwardly and with curious tokens of affection.

METHODS OF ESCAPING LOVE When a person wishes to run away from love, he sometimes does it by leaning over backwards and making it appear that he may have not only neutral but even hostile feelings toward another person. The very things he most loves and cherishes are the things he depreciates. Just as a gem merchant may depreciate the cut of a stone or the setting of a ring he hopes to purchase at a reduced price, so some persons hide their attitudes of love by critical comments. The surest token of a mother's rejection of a child is her criticism of him, but criticism may also imply a degree of fondness. A person must have some positive feeling toward the other or he could not even care enough to criticize him. The wife who finds fault with her husband because he does not groom himself properly or use sufficient tact in his business dealings does so, not only because of an underlying hostility, but also because she loves him and wants to help him. The "sour grapes" rationalization is frequently the depreciation of the very thing that is most desired.

Some persons escape loving by adopting a style of life that removes them from contact with others. A man may choose a vocation in which he works alone rather than with others. A woman may isolate herself by choosing to teach in an institution or a remote community where she is removed from contacts. The adolescent boy or girl may avoid the groups, cliques, clubs, or fraternities in which he would find relationships and prefer to go his own way as a "lone wolf."

Some persons escape intimate contacts by assuming obligations and duties which confine them. A woman may accept the responsibility for the care of an aged mother or father or responsibility for putting a brother or sister through college. This very responsibility ties her down and removes her from associations with those of her own age and interests. Many a man has been prevented from courting a girl who seems always to be engaged with some responsibility which leaves her no freedom.

Another way of escaping love is by demanding too much of the other person. A man may demand beauty in his wife, or a wife may demand wealth in her husband. When the other person is wanted for something that he owns or for some special quality, he is not wanted for himself but in order to provide special gratification.

Values of Object Love

Love has become the foundation of the Christian religion and is extolled and glorified by everyone old and young. Love is the basis for the most profound happiness human beings are capable of achieving. One's love relations are cherished as experiences of paramount value. If one looks back over the years, his comings and goings, his achievements and successes pale in significance beside the memories of companionships and intimate associations with others.

The richest life is that which is filled with associations with others. Anyone who writes an autobiography entitled, *Across the Busy Years*, records not only his achievements but also his associations and intimate relations with others. A life filled with personal worthwhile contacts is one based on love. Love provides the surest guarantee of security from fear. One can best protect himself from disturbing anxieties when he is secure in the gift of his love to another person. The person who loves becomes relaxed and at ease and is able to throw off the burden of tension. Love helps a person to achieve peace of mind and freedom from guilt. The person in love is assured of his potency. The capacity to achieve and the capacity to love and to understand are the two principal weapons or tools for the conquest of, and adjustment to, the external world. Love frees one from crippling dependency on others and from sensitivity to criticism, scorn, and contempt. Love is a successful solution to the threat of loneliness and isolation. Many persons are afraid really to accept pleasure and enjoyment for themselves because of crippling experiences in dark years. The highest form of pleasure comes to the person who is able to give himself in love.

Love is the essence of desirable group life. The world today is struggling to recover from a global conflict which has brought misery and terror to most peoples. Efforts are being made to create a world in which this misery will never have to be repeated. In a previous chapter the cause of war was found to lie in aggressive tendencies in man; the basis for peace, on the other hand, must be found in the love tendencies in man. Somehow love tendencies must be provided with an opportunity for expression, and a world organization must be established which can foster the love impulse. Love in the last analysis is the only antidote for hate.

Love is the strongest civilizing factor. There is no doubt that love occupies a more important place in world affairs today than in any time in previous history. It is certain that men are more sensitive to cruelty, to slavery, and to torture and that they hate these things more today than ever before. We have a clearer notion of what kind of world we would like to live in and we have a dim insight as to how this kind of world can be accomplished. The force which has helped men grow out of barbarism is love. Love brings a change from egoism to altruism. It is love that enables men to live collectively, to care for one another, and to establish arrangements for social security.

Love is the basis for emotional security and stability in the individual. It is love from the parents that helps to establish the secure personality in infancy, and the emotionally stable adult is one who has been loved by fond parents in early life. Parents can never love a child too much or too well.

Love is the basis for effective personality development. The finest individuals are those who have been nourished in an atmosphere of love.

Educational Implications

USE OF LOVE IN LEARNING   Theories of learning have stressed the importance of satisfaction as a factor in the learning process. Children learn better by praise than by blame or indifference. Praise even in mild degree is an expression of love. Children learn most readily in response to love. Anna Freud, for instance, has noted the fact, many times verified, that the most important motive for the learning in school is love of the teacher. Children are motivated less by prizes, competition, and other extraneous incentives than they are by wishing to please the teacher and secure some token of affection from her. Teachers and parents recognize that the threat of the withdrawal of love is the most potent form of punishment. In fact, it is so devastating that it may have disastrous and traumatic effects if used too severely. Parents or nurses who threaten the child with the bogeyman or the policeman or say that they will go away and never come back are creating deep wounds in the child's security and erecting barriers to the child's possibilities of growing toward emotional maturity.

LOVE AS A GROWTH PROCESS AND PRODUCT OF MATURITY Love is a growth process and is not something that reaches full maturity at once. Two persons who marry should recognize that the first flush of physical attraction is far from being the full fruition of love impulses. Love is something that matures as a result of years of mutual cooperation, mutual enjoyment, and mutual suffering. As individuals share experiences with one another they are providing a broader and sounder basis for love.

Therapeutic Implications of Love

Those whose task it is to help distressed persons back to more normal living find that the key to the difficulty frequently is the person's ability to accept himself. The neurotic individual needs self-love in order to become well. A wise counselor will use every opportunity for ego building, for making a person feel greater respect and pleasure in himself. Self-respect is the basis on which all good adjustment must be founded.

The aim in therapy is not to destroy narcissism or self-love where it is too intense but to dilute and dissolve it. The patient must find it possible to relax the tight grasp on himself and by slow degrees give of himself to others. As the individual through the security in a personal relationship dares to venture out and give himself to others, he will find the path for the return to health.

On the other hand, therapy fails when narcissism is strong. When the individual is unable to establish a relationship with others, there is no means with which constructive influences can be put into operation.

The overnarcissistic person who is wrapped up in his own experiences and pleasures can seldom establish a secure relationship with another person, and where a relationship does develop it is likely to be of an exceedingly infantile and dependent nature, demanding and consuming in its nature. It is for this reason that therapeutic methods promise considerable help to those who are afflicted with the transference neuroses, but their use in aiding individuals with various forms of narcissistic neuroses is more difficult. Freud in his early practice found that love, particularly sexual love, could serve as a kind of resistance and hence impede the process of psychoanalytic treatment. If a relationship becomes all important to an individual, the individual's attention may be diverted from understanding and development of the self to an exaggerated interest in the person or the counselor. Freud's warning in this instance is that the counselor make sure that he himself is not involved emotionally in the relationship and that he keep his attention focused on an understanding and interpretation of the meaning of the experience to the client rather than to accept it or oppose it emotionally.

The wise counselor is one who avoids giving direct advice with regard to love relationships and concentrates his efforts on breaking down the barriers which make these relationships difficult or distorted. Rickman holds that a counselor would be unwise to advise marriage or sex relations as a therapeutic measure. If there is difficulty along these lines, it has a psychological basis, and this needs to be worked through first. As he points out, the sexual impulse is in every instance so demanding and outgoing that there is no need to give it special encouragement; but if for some reason it is blocked, the primary need is to knock down the psychological barriers and resistances. Psychotherapy aims to release hostile impulses so as to dissipate them and permit the love impulses to break through into open expression and to assist them to mature and become firmly established.

A. H. MASLOW

Love in Healthy People*

This contribution was written at the request of the editor for a symposium entitled
The Meaning of Love. *In a slightly revised version, under the title "Love in*
Self-Actualizing People," it forms a chapter in Maslow's Motivation and
Personality.[1]

Maslow here provides an elaborate and largely successful description of mature
love. His conclusions are based on a study of a large number of students and other
persons. Hence, his investigation represents one of the first, if not the first, studies on
human beings with the object of throwing light on the nature of mental health. By
"self-actualization" Maslow meant behavior designed to achieve "the full use and
exploitation of talents, capacities, potentialities, etc." It is refreshing, where so many
have paid attention to the genesis and relationships of love in the infant and young,
to have a good operational description of love in adults.

A defect, perhaps, of Maslow's study is that he does not tell us anything about
sex differences and, indeed, seems uninterested in them. But clearly he writes from a
largely masculine point of view, though a very humane and embracing one.

Maslow points out that spontaneity and gaiety are omitted by Fromm and Adler
from their conceptions of love; thus his ideas conform to our definition of mental
health as the ability to love, to work, and to play—the last is too often omitted from
the list of criteria defining mental health. In a healthy love relationship, however, it
is an indispensable condition, principally in the form of a sense of humor, the
balance-wheel of character.

It is amazing how little the empirical sciences have to offer on the
subject of love. Particularly strange is the silence of the psychologists,

"Love in Healthy People" by A. H. Maslow. From Ashley Montagu, ed., *The Meaning of Love* (New York: The Julian Press, Inc., 1953), pp. 57–93. Reprinted by permission of Ashley Montagu.

* Numbers in brackets in the text refer to bibliographical references at the end of this
chapter.
[1] New York: Harper & Row, rev. ed., 1970, pp. 181–202.

for one might think this to be their particular obligation. Probably this is just another example of the besetting sin of the academicians, that they prefer to do what they are easily able rather than what they ought, like the kitchen helper I knew who opened every can in the hotel one day because he was so *very* good at opening cans.

Sometimes this is merely sad or irritating, as in the case of the textbooks of psychology and sociology, practically none of which treats the subject. The only real exceptions I have found are Symonds' *Dynamics of Human Adjustment* and various writings of Sorokin, of which the latest is a symposium, *Explorations in Altruistic Love and Behavior.*

More often the situation becomes completely ludicrous. One might reasonably expect that writers of serious treatises on the family, on marriage, and on sex should consider the subject of love to be a proper, even basic, part of their self-imposed task. But I must report that no single one of the volumes on these subjects available in the library where I work has any serious mention of the subject. More often, the word "love" is not even indexed.

I must confess that I understand this better now that I have undertaken the task myself. It is an extraordinarily difficult subject to handle in any tradition. And it is triply so in the scientific tradition. It is as if we were at the most advanced position in no-man's-land, at a point where the conventional techniques of orthodox psychological science are of very little use.

And yet our duty is clear. We *must* understand love; we must be able to teach it, to create it, to predict it, or else the world is lost to hostility and to suspicion. [3] The importance of the goal lends worth and dignity even to such unreliable data as are herein offered. Furthermore they are, so far as I know, the only "data" available on the subject.

The principle upon which the research proceeded was simple enough, however difficult it turned out to be in practice. On the basis of the psychiatric and psychological knowledge now available, I tried to find actual cases of psychiatric health from among all the people I knew or had heard of or had read about. They turned out to be extremely rare. I was able to turn up only about five to forty, depending on the rigor of my criteria, and the inclusion of doubtful and insufficiently known people. This was supplemented by studies with college students. No single one of about 4,000 students could be said to be truly self-actualizing, but the top one or two percent—in terms of healthiness—were selected out for testing and study. This research is still in progress.

This study is pre-scientific rather than scientific in the ordinary sense. And yet the writer consoles himself with the fact that the shortcomings of this report arise out of intrinsic difficulties of the task and of the material rather than out of neglect, laziness, or carelessness. Probing and questioning are severely limited when one deals with people who (a) are older than the questioner and (b) have a much stronger sense of privacy than the average person. I learned early that I had to get my data indirectly rather than directly, subtly rather than bluntly, and that often it came in an equivocal form which I had to "interpret." I felt often like a detective working with circumstantial evidence rather than with eye-witness reports.

But all these difficulties become even more weighty when we deal with sex, love, and marriage. In this area my reticent subjects outdid themselves, and I must henceforth speak of "impressions" rather than of data.

The possibilities for projection of the investigator's own attitudes are obvious, and it is only fair to warn my readers about this source of unreliability. Various other difficulties of sampling and of statistics have been presented in my original report on self-actualizing (psychiatrically healthy) people. [22] The reader is referred to this paper for the background of the present report, as well as for the possible criticisms of it.

1. A Preliminary Description of Some Characteristics of Love between the Sexes

We shall mention first some of the better-known characteristics of love between the sexes and then proceed to the more special findings of our study of self-actualizing people. A very useful description to start with is available in Symonds' chapter on "Love and Self-Love" in his *Dynamics of Human Adjustment.* [34]

The core of the description of love must be subjective or phenomenological rather than objective or behavioral. No description, no words can ever communicate the full quality of the love experience to one who has himself never felt it. It consists primarily of a feeling of tenderness and affection with great enjoyment, happiness, and satisfaction in experiencing this feeling (if all is going well). There is a tendency to want to get closer, to come into more intimate contact, to touch and embrace the loved person, to yearn for him. This person furthermore is perceived in some desirable way, whether as beautiful, as good, or as attractive; in any case, there is pleasure in looking at and being with the loved one and distress in separation from him. Perhaps from this comes the tendency to focus attention upon the loved person, along with the tendency to forget other people, and to narrow perception in such a way that many things are not noticed. It is as if the loved person were in himself attractive, and *pulled* the attention and perception of the loving person. This feeling of pleasure in contact and in being with, shows itself also in the desire to be together with the loved one as much as possible in as many situations as possible: in work, in play, during esthetic and intellectual pursuits. There is often expressed a desire to share pleasant experiences with the loved person so that it is often reported that the pleasant experience is more pleasant because of the presence of the sweetheart.

Finally, of course, there is a special sexual arousal in the lover. This, in the typical instance, shows itself directly in genital changes. The beloved person seems to have a special power that nobody else in the world has to the same degree of producing erection and secretion in the partner, of arousing specific conscious sexual desire, and of producing the usual pricklings and tinglings that go with sexual arousal. And yet this is not essential, since love can be observed in people who are too old for sexual intercourse.

The desire for intimacy is not only physical but also psychological. It expresses itself frequently as a special taste for privacy for the pair. In addition to this, I have observed often the growth in a pair who love each other of a secret language, secret sexual words which other people can't understand, and of special tricks and gestures which only the lovers understand.

Quite characteristic is the feeling of generosity, of wanting to give and to please. The lover gets special pleasure from doing things for and making gifts to the loved one.

Very common is the desire for a fuller knowledge of one another, a yearning for a kind of psychological intimacy and psychological proximity and of being fully known to each other. Special delight in sharing secrets is common. Perhaps these are sub-examples which come under the broader heading of personality fusion of which we shall speak below.

A common example of the tendency to generosity and to do things for the one who is loved are the very common fantasies in which a person will imagine himself making great sacrifices for the sake of his sweetheart.

2. *Dropping of Defenses in Self-actualizing*
Love Relationships

Theodor Reik [27, p. 171] has defined one characteristic of love as the absence of anxiety. This is seen with exceptional clearness in healthy individuals. There is little question about the tendency to more and more complete spontaneity, the dropping of defenses, the dropping of roles, and of trying and striving in the relationship. As the relationship continues, there is a growing intimacy and honesty and self-expression, which at its height is a rare phenomenon. The report from these people is that with a beloved person it is possible to be oneself, to feel natural; "I can let my hair down." This honesty also includes allowing one's faults, weaknesses, and physical and psychological shortcomings to be freely seen by the partner.

There is much less tendency to put the best foot forward in the healthy love relationship. This goes so far as to make less likely the hiding even of physical defects of middle and old age, of false teeth, braces, girdles, and the like. There is much less maintenance of distance, mystery, and glamour, much less reserve and concealment and secrecy. This complete dropping of the guard definitely contradicts folk wisdom on the subject, not to mention some of the psychoanalytic theorists. For instance, Reik believes that being a good pal and being a good sweetheart are mutually exclusive and contradictory. Our data seem to indicate the contrary.

Our data definitely contradict also the age-old "intrinsic hostility between the sexes" theory. This hostility between the sexes, this suspicion of the opposite sex, this tendency to identify with one's own sex in an alliance against the other sex, even the very phrasing itself of "opposite sex" is found often enough in neurotic people and even in average citizens in our society, but it is definitely not found in self-actualizing people, at least with the resources for research that I had at my disposal.

Another finding that contradicts folk wisdom and also some of the more esoteric theorists on sexuality and love, for example, Guyon, is the definite finding that in self-actualizing people the love satisfactions and the sex satisfactions both improve with the age of the relationship. It is a very common report from these individuals that "sex is better than it used to be" and "seems to be improving all the time." It seems quite clear that even the strictly sensual and physical satisfactions are improved by familiarity with the partner rather than by novelty in healthy people. Of course, there is little doubt that novelty in the sexual partner is very exciting and attractive, especially for definitely neurotic people, but our data make it very unwise to make any generalization about this, and certainly not for self-actualizing people.

We may sum up this characteristic of self-actualizing love in the generalization that healthy love is in part an absence of defenses, that is to say, an increase in spontaneity and in honesty. The healthy love relationship tends to make it possible for two people to be spontaneous, to know each other and still to love each other. Of course, this implies that as one gets to know another person more and more intimately and profoundly, one will like what one sees. If the partner is profoundly "bad" rather than "good," then increasing familiarity will produce not increasing preference but increasing antagonism and revulsion. This reminds me of a finding that I made in a little study of the effects of familiarization on paintings. My finding was that "good" paintings become more and more preferred and enjoyed with increasing familiarization, but that "bad" paintings become less and less preferred. The difficulty of deciding at that time on some objective criterion of "good" and "bad" in paintings was so great that I preferred not to publish the finding. But if I may be permitted this amount of subjectivism, then I will say that the "better" people are, the more they will be loved with greater familiarity; the "worse" people are (by my standards) then the *less* they will be liked as familiarity increases.

One of the deepest satisfactions coming from the healthy love relationship reported by my subjects is that such a relationship permits the greatest spontaneity, the greatest naturalness, the greatest dropping of defenses and protection against threat. In such a relationship it is not necessary to be guarded, to conceal, to try to impress, to feel tense, to watch one's words or actions, to suppress or repress. My people report that they can be themselves without feeling that there are demands or expectations upon them; they can feel psychologically (as well as physically) naked and still feel loved and wanted and secure.

Rogers has described this well. [28, p. 159] " 'Loved' has here perhaps its deepest and most general meaning—that of being deeply understood and deeply accepted. . . . We can love a person only to the extent that we are not threatened by him; we can love only if his reactions to us, or to those things which affect us, are understandable to us. . . . Thus, if a person is hostile toward me, and I can see nothing in him at the moment except the hostility, I am quite sure that I will react in a defensive way to the hostility."

Menninger [24] describes the reverse side of the coin. "Love is impaired less by the feeling that we are not appreciated than by a dread, more or less dimly felt by everyone, lest others see through our masks, the masks of repression that have been forced upon us by convention and culture. It is this that leads us to shun intimacy, to maintain friendships on a superficial level, to underestimate and fail to appreciate others lest they come to appreciate us too well."

3. The Ability to Love and to Be Loved

My subjects were loved and were loving and are loved and are loving. In practically all (not quite all) my subjects where data were available, this tended to point to the conclusion that (all other things being equal) psychological health comes from being loved rather than from being deprived of love. [19, 22] Granted that the ascetic path is a possible one, and that frustration has some good effects; yet basic need-gratification seems to be much more the usual precursor or *Anlage* of health. This seems to be true not only for being loved but for loving as well. (That *other* requirements are also necessary is proven by the psychopathic personality, especially as exemplified by Levy's [18] indulged psychopath.)

It is also true of our self-actualizing people that they *now* love and are loved. For certain reasons it had better be said that they have the power to love and the ability to *be* loved. (Even though this may sound like a repetition of the sentence before, it really is not.) These are clinically observed facts, and are quite public and easily repeatable.

Menninger [24] makes the very acute statement that human beings really *do* want to love each other but just don't know how to go about it. This is much less true for healthy people. *They* at least know how to love, and can do so freely and easily and naturally and without getting wound up in conflicts or threats or inhibitions.

However, my subjects used the word "love" warily and with circumspection. They applied it only to a few rather than to many, tending to distinguish sharply between loving someone and liking him or being friendly or benevolent or brotherly. It describes for them an intense feeling, not a mild or disinterested one.

4. Sexuality in Self-actualizing Love

We can learn a very great deal from the peculiar and complex nature of sex in the love-life of self-actualizing people. It is by no means a simple story; there are many interwoven threads. On the whole, however, their sex life is characteristic and can be described in such a way as to make possible various conclusions, both positive and negative, about the nature of sex as well as about the nature of love.

For one thing it can be reported that sex and love can be and most often are very perfectly fused with each other in healthy people. While it is perfectly true that these are separable concepts, and while no purpose would be served in confusing them with each other unnecessarily [27, 33], still it must be reported that in the life of healthy people, they tend to become completely joined and merged with each other. As a matter of fact we may also say that they become less separable and less separate from each other in the lives of the people we have studied. We cannot go so far as some who say that any person who is capable of having sexual pleasure where there is no love must be a sick man. But we can certainly go in this direction. It is certainly fair to say that self-actualizing men and women tend on the whole not to seek sex for its own sake, or to be satisfied with it alone when it comes. I am not sure that my data permit me to say that they would rather not have sex at all if it came without affection, but I am quite sure that I have many instances in which for the time being at least sex was given up or rejected because it came without love and affection.

Another finding already reported [22] is the very strong impression that the sexual pleasures are found in their most intense and ecstatic perfection in self-actualizing people. If love is a yearning for the perfect and for complete fusion, then the orgasm as sometimes reported by self-actualizing people becomes the attainment of it. Experiences described in reports that I have obtained have indeed been at so great a level of intensity that I felt it justifiable to record them as "mystic experiences." Such phrases as "too big to assimilate," "too good to be true," "too good to last," etc., have been coupled with reports of being swept away completely by forces beyond control. This combination of very perfect and intense sexuality along with other characteristics to be reported produces several seeming paradoxes which I now wish to discuss.[1]

In self-actualizing people the orgasm is simultaneously more impor-

---

[1] Oswald Schwarz, *The Psychology of Sex* (Harmondsworth, Middlesex: Penguin Books, 1951), p. 21: "Although totally different in nature, sexual impulse and love are dependent on, and complementary to, each other. *In a perfect, fully mature human being only this inseparable fusion of sexual impulse and love exists.* This is the fundamental principle of any psychology of sex. If there be anyone capable of experiencing the purely physical gratification of sex, he is stigmatized as sexually subnormal (immature or otherwise)."

tant and less important than in average people. It is often a profound and almost mystical experience, and yet the absence of sexuality is more easily tolerated by these people. This is not a paradox or a contradiction. It follows from dynamic motivation theory. Living at a higher need level makes the lower needs and their frustrations and satisfactions less important, less central, more easily neglected. But it also makes them more wholeheartedly enjoyed when gratified. [23]

An excellent parallel may be made between this and the attitude of these people toward food. Food is simultaneously enjoyed and yet regarded as relatively unimportant in the total scheme of life by self-actualizing people. When they do enjoy it, they can enjoy it whole-heartedly and without the slightest tainting with bad attitudes toward animality and the like. And yet ordinarily feeding oneself takes a relatively unimportant place in the total picture. These people do not *need* sensuality; they simply enjoy it when it occurs.

Certainly also food takes a relatively unimportant place in the philosophy of Utopia, in Heaven, in the good life, in the philosophy of values and ethics. It is something basic, to be taken for granted, to be used as a foundation stone upon which higher things are built. These people are very ready to recognize that the higher things cannot be built until the lower ones are built, but once these lower needs are satisfied, they recede from consciousness, and there is little preoccupation with them.

The same seems to be true for sex. Sex can be, as I said, whole-heartedly enjoyed, enjoyed far beyond the possibility of the average person, even at the same time that it does not play any central role in the philosophy of life. It is something to be enjoyed, something to be taken for granted, something to build upon, something that is very basically important like water or food, and which can be enjoyed as much as these; but gratification should be taken for granted. I think such an attitude as this resolves the apparent paradox in the self-actualizing person's simultaneously enjoying sex so much more intensely than the average person, yet at the same time considering it so much less important in the total frame of reference.

It should be stressed that from this same complex attitude toward sex arises the fact that the orgasm may bring on mystical experiences, and yet at other times may be taken rather lightly. This is to say that the sexual pleasure of self-actualizing people may be very intense or not intense at all. This conflicts with the romantic attitude that "love is a divine rapture, a transport, a mystic experience." It is true that it may be also a delicate pleasure rather than an intense one, a gay and light-hearted, playful sort of thing rather than a serious and profound experience or even a neutral duty. These people do not always live on the heights—they may live at a more average level of intensity, and lightly and mildly enjoy sex as a titillating, pleasant, playful, enjoyable, tickling kind of experience instead of a plumbing of the most intense depths of ecstatic emotionality. This is especially true when the subjects are relatively fatigued. Under such circumstances, the lighter kind of sex may take place.

Self-actualizing love shows many of the characteristics of self-actualization in general. For instance, one characteristic is that it is based on a healthy acceptance of the self and of others. So much can be accepted by these people that others would not accept. For example, in spite of the fact that these people are relatively more monogamous than the average, and relatively less driven to love affairs outside the marriage, yet they are much more free than the average to admit to the fact of sexual attraction to others. My impression is that there tends to be a rather easy relationship with the opposite sex, along with casual acceptance of the phenomenon of being attracted to other people, at the same time that these individuals do rather less about this attraction than other people. Also it seems to me that their talk about sex is considerably more free and casual and unconventional than the average. Now what this sums up to is an acceptance of the facts of life, which, going along with the more intense and profound and satisfying love relationship, seems to make it less *necessary* to seek for compensatory or neurotic sex affairs outside the marriage. This is an interesting instance in which acceptance and behavior do not correlate. The easier acceptance of the facts of sexuality seems to make it easier rather than harder to be relatively monogamous.

In one instance, where the woman had long since separated from her husband, whatever information I was able to get from her indicated that she went in for what would be called promiscuity. She had sexual affairs and was very definite about how she enjoyed them. This was a fifty-five-year-old woman. I was never able to get more details than her statements that she did have such affairs and that she enjoyed sex very much. There was no slight element of guilt or anxiety or of the feeling of doing anything wrong in her conversation about this matter. Apparently the tendency to monogamy is not the same as the tendency to chastity, or a rejection of sexuality. It is just that the more profoundly satisfying the love relationship, the less necessity there is for all sorts of compulsions for sex affairs with people other than the wife or husband.

Of course, this acceptance of sexuality is also a main basis for the intensity of enjoyment of sexuality which I find in self-actualizing people. Another characteristic I found of love in healthy people is that they made no really sharp differentiation between the roles and personalities of the two sexes. That is, they did not assume that the female was passive and the male active, whether in sex or love or anything else. These people were all so certain of their maleness or femaleness that they did not mind taking on some of the cultural aspects of the opposite sex role. It was especially noteworthy that they could be both active and passive lovers and this was clearest in the sexual act and in physical love-making. Kissing and being kissed, being above or below in the sexual act, taking the initiative, being quiet and receiving love, teasing and being teased—these were all found in both sexes. The report indicated that both were enjoyed at different times. It was considered to be a shortcoming to be limited to just active love-making or passive love-making. Both have their particular pleasures for self-actualizing people.

This can go pretty far, almost to the point of reminding us of sadism and masochism. There can be a joy in being used, in subjection and passivity, even in accepting pain, in being exploited. Also, there can be an active and positive pleasure in squeezing and hugging and biting and in being violent and even in inflicting and receiving pain, so long as this does not get out of bounds.

Here again we have an instance of the way in which common dichotomies are so often resolved in self-actualization, appearing to be valid dichotomies only because people are not healthy enough.

This agrees with D'Arcy's [6] thesis that erotic and agapean love are basically different but merge in the best people. He speaks about two kinds of love which are ultimately masculine or feminine, active or passive, self-centered or self-effacing, and it is true that in the general run of the public these seem to contrast and be at opposite poles. However, it is different in healthy people. In these individuals the dichotomies are resolved, and the individual becomes both active and passive, both selfish and unselfish, both masculine and feminine, both self-interested and self-effacing. D'Arcy acknowledges that this occurs with extreme rarity.

One negative conclusion that our data, limited though they are, permit us to make with considerable confidence is that the Freudian tendency to derive love from sex or to identify them is a bad mistake.[2]

[2] M. Balint, "On Genital Love," *International Journal of Psychoanalysis*, 29 (1948), 34–40: "If one reads the psychoanalytical literature for references to genital love, to one's surprise two

Of course Freud is not alone in this error—it is shared by many less thoughtful citizens—but he may be taken as its most influential exponent in Western civilization. There are traces here and there in Freud's writings that he had different thoughts about the matter occasionally. Once, for example, he spoke about the child's feeling for the mother as deriving from the "self-preservation" instincts, i.e., a kind of feeling akin to gratitude for being fed and cared for: "It [affection] springs from the very earliest years of childhood, and was formed on the foundation provided by the interests of the self-preservation instinct." [9, p. 204] In another place he interprets it as reaction formation [p. 252]; again, as the "mental side of the sexual impulse." [p. 259]

On the whole, however, the most widely accepted of the various theories put forth by Freud is the following: Tenderness is "aim-inhibited sexuality." [3] That is, to put it very bluntly, it is deflected and disguised sexuality. When we are forbidden to fulfill the sexual "aim" of coupling, and when we keep on wanting to and don't dare admit to ourselves that we are, then the compromise product is tenderness and affection. Contrariwise, whenever we meet with tenderness and affection we have no Freudian recourse but to regard this as "aim-inhibited" sexuality. Another deduction from this premise that seems unavoidable is that if sex were never inhibited, and if everyone could couple with anyone else, then there would be no tender love. Incest taboos and repression—these are what breed love. For other views see our bibliography. [4, 5, 17, 29]

Another kind of love discussed by the Freudians is "genital love," frequently defined with exclusive emphasis on "genital" and without any reference to "love." For instance, it is often defined as the power to be potent, to have a good orgasm, to have this orgasm from penile-vaginal coupling without the *necessity* of recourse to clitoris, anus,

striking facts emerge: (a) much less has been written on genital love than on pre-genital love; (b) almost everything that has been written on genital love is negative." See also Balint, M., "The Final Goal of Psychoanalytic Treatment," *International Journal of Psychoanalysis*, 17 (1936), 206.

[3] Sigmund Freud, *Civilization and Its Discontents*: "These people make themselves independent of their object's acquiescence by transferring the main value from the fact of being loved to their own act of loving; they protect themselves against loss of it by attaching their love not to individual objects but to all men equally, and they avoid the uncertainties and disappointments of genital love by turning away from its sexual aim and modifying the instinct into an impulse with an *inhibited aim*. The state which they induce in themselves by this process—an unchangeable, undeviating, tender attitude—has little superficial likeness to the stormy vicissitudes of genital love, from which it is nevertheless derived."

sadism, masochism, etc. The best statement in the Freudian tradition I have been able to find is the one by Michael Balint.[4]

How tenderness is involved in genital love remains a mystery, for in sexual intercourse there is, of course, no inhibition of the sexual aim (it *is* the sexual aim). Nothing has been said by Freud of aim-*gratified* sexuality. If tenderness is found in genital love, then some source other than aim-inhibition must be found, a non-sexual source, it would seem. Suttie's analysis [33] very effectively reveals the weaknesses of this position. So also do those of Reik [27], Fromm [13, 14], DeForest [7], and others in the revisionist-Freudian tradition. Adler [2] in 1908 affirmed that the need for affection was not derived from sex.

5. Care, Responsibility, the Pooling of Needs

One important aspect of a good love relationship is what may be called need-identification or the pooling of the hierarchies of basic needs in two persons into a single hierarchy. The effect of this is that one person feels another's needs as if they were his own and for that

[4] "On Genital Love": "To avoid this pitfall [emphasis on negative qualities] let us examine an ideal case of such postambivalent genital love that has no traces of ambivalency and in addition no traces of pre-genital object relationship; (a) there should be no greediness, no insatiability, no wish to devour the object, to deny it any independent existence, i.e., there should be no oral features; (b) there should be no wish to hurt, to humiliate, to boss, to dominate the object, etc., i.e., no sadistic features; (c) there should be no wish to defile the partner, to despise him (her) for his (her) sexual desires and pleasures. There should be no danger of being disgusted by the partner or being attracted only by some unpleasant features of him, etc., and there should be no remnants of anal traits; (D) there should be no compulsion to boast about the possession of a penis, no fear of the partner's sexual organs, no fear for one's own sexual organs, no envy of the male or female genitalia, no feeling of being incomplete or of having a faulty sexual organ, or of the partner having a faulty one, etc. There should be no trace of the phallic phase or of the castration complex. . . . What is then 'genital love' apart from the absence of all the enumerated pregenital traits? Well, we love our partner (1) because he or she can satisfy us; (2) because we can satisfy him or her; because we can experience a full orgasm together nearly or quite simultaneously. . . . Genital satisfaction is apparently only a necessary and not a sufficient condition of genital love. What we have learned is that genital love is much more than gratitude for or contentment about the partner being available for genital satisfaction. Further that it does not make any difference whether this gratitude or contentment is onesided or mutual. What is this? We find in addition to the genital satisfaction in a true love relation (1) idealization; (2) tenderness; (3) a special form of identification. To sum up: Genital love in man is really a misnomer. . . . What we call genital love is a fusion of disagreeing elements, genital satisfaction and pregenital tenderness . . . the reward for fearing the strain of this fusion is the possibility of regressing periodically for some happy moments to a really infantile stage of *no* reality testing. . . ."

matter also feels his own needs to some extent as if they belonged to the other. An ego now expands to cover two people, and to some extent the two people have become for psychological purposes a single unit, a single person, a single ego.

This principle, probably first presented in technical form by Alfred Adler [2, 8, 35], has been very well phrased by Erich Fromm [14], particularly in his book *Man for Himself,* in which love is defined as follows: "Love, in principle, is indivisible as far as the connection between 'objects' and one's own self is concerned. Genuine love is an expression of productiveness and implies care, respect, responsibility, and knowledge. It is not an 'affect' in the sense of being affected by somebody, an active striving for the growth and happiness of the loved person, rooted in one's own capacity to love" (pp. 129–130).

Schlick [30, p. 186] has also phrased this well: "The social impulses are those dispositions of a person by virtue of which the idea of a pleasant or unpleasant state of *another* person is itself a pleasant or unpleasant experience (also the mere perception of another creature, his presence alone, can, by virtue of such an impulse, elicit feelings of pleasure). The natural effect of these inclinations is that their bearer establishes the joyful states of others as ends of his conduct. And, upon realization of these ends he enjoys the resultant pleasure; for not only the idea, but also the actual perception of the expression of joy pleases him."

The ordinary way in which this need-identification shows itself to the eyes of the world is in terms of taking on responsibility, of care, of concern for another person. The loving husband can get as much pleasure from his wife's pleasure as he can from his own. The loving mother would much rather cough herself than hear her child cough, and as a matter of fact would willingly take on to her own shoulders the disease of her child, since it would be less painful for her to have it than to see and hear her child have it. A good example of this is seen in the differential reactions in good marriages and bad marriages to illness and the consequently necessary nursing. An illness in the good couple is an illness of the couple rather than a misfortune of one of the pair. Equal responsibility is automatically taken, and it is as if they were both simultaneously struck. The primitive communism of the loving family shows itself in this way and not only in the sharing of food or of money. It is here that one sees at its best and purest the exemplification of the principle: from each according to his abilities and to each according to his needs. The only modification that is here necessary is that the needs of the other person *are* the needs of the lover.

If the relationship is a very good one, then the sick or weak one can throw himself upon the nursing care and the protectiveness of the loving partner with the same abandonment and lack of threat and lack of self-consciousness that a child shows in falling asleep in his parent's arms. It is often enough observed in less healthy couples that illness makes a strain in the couple. For the strong man whose masculinity is practically identified with physical strength, illness and weakness is a catastrophe and so is it also for his wife if she has defined masculinity in the same way. For the woman who defines femininity in terms of physical attractiveness of the beauty contest style, then illness or weakness or anything else that lessens her physical attractiveness is for her a tragedy, and for the man as well if he defines femininity in the same way. Our healthy people are almost completely exempted from this mistake.

If we remember that human beings are in the last analysis isolated from each other and encapsulated, each one in his own little shell, and if we agree that also in the last analysis people can never really know each other as they know themselves, then every intercourse between groups and individuals is like an effort of "two solitudes to protect, and touch and greet each other" (Rilke). Of all such efforts that we know anything about, the healthy love relationship is the most effective way of bridging the unbridgable gap between two separate human beings.

In the history of theorizing about love relations as well as about altruism, patriotism, etc., much has been said about the transcendence of the ego. An excellent modern discussion of this tendency at the technical level is afforded in a book by Angyal [1], in which he discusses various examples of a tendency to what he calls heteronomy, and which he contrasts with the tendency to autonomy, to independence, to individuality, and the like. More and more clinical and historical evidence accumulates to indicate that Angyal is right in demanding that some room be made in a systematic psychology for these various tendencies to go out beyond the limits of the ego. Furthermore, it seems quite clear that this need to go out beyond the limits of the ego may be a need in the same sense that we have needs for vitamins and minerals, i.e., that if the need is not satisfied, the person becomes sick in one way or another. I should say that the most satisfying and most complete example of ego transcendence, and certainly the most healthy from the point of view of avoiding illness of the character, is the throwing of oneself into a healthy love relationship.

6. Fun and Gaiety in the Healthy Love
Relationship

The concepts of Erich Fromm and Alfred Adler which were mentioned above stress productiveness, care, responsibility. This is all very true, but Fromm, Adler, and the others who write in the same vein strangely omit one aspect of the healthy love relationship which was very clear in my subjects: namely, fun, merriment, gaiety. It is quite characteristic of self-actualizing people that they can enjoy themselves in love and in sex. Sex very frequently becomes a kind of a game in which laughter is quite as common as panting. The way in which Fromm and other serious thinkers on the subject have described the ideal love relationship is to make it into something of a task or a burden rather than a game or a pleasure. When Fromm [14, p. 110] says: "Love is the productive form of relatedness to others and to oneself. It implies responsibility, care, respect and knowledge, and the wish for the other person to grow and develop. It is the expression of intimacy between two human beings under the condition of the preservation of each other's integrity"; it must be admitted that this sounds a little like a pact or a partnership of some kind, rather than a spontaneous sportiveness. It is not the welfare of the species, or the task of reproduction, or the future development of mankind that attracts people to each other. The sex life of healthy people, in spite of the fact that it frequently reaches great peaks of ecstasy, is nevertheless also easily compared to the games of children and puppies. It is cheerful, humorous, and playful. We shall point out in greater detail below that it is not primarily a striving, as Fromm implies; it is basically an enjoyment and a delight, which is another thing altogether.

7. Acceptance of the Other's Individuality;
Respect for the Other

All serious writers on the subject of ideal or healthy love have stressed the affirmation of the other's individuality, the eagerness for the growth of the other, the essential respect for his individuality and unique personality. This is confirmed very strongly by the observation of self-actualizing people, who have in unusual measure the rare ability to be pleased rather than threatened by the partner's triumphs. They do indeed respect their partners in a very profound and basic way which has many, many implications. As Overstreet says quite well [26,

p. 103], "The love of a person implies, not the possession of that person, but the affirmation of that person. It means granting him, gladly, the full right to his unique manhood."

Fromm's statement on the subject is also very impressive [13, p. 261]: "Love is the foremost component of such spontaneity; not love as the dissolution of the self in another person, but love as a spontaneous affirmation of others, as the union of the individual with others on the basis of the preservation of the individual himself." A most impressive example of this respect is the ungrudging pride of such a man in his wife's achievements, even where they outshine his. Another is the absence of jealousy.

This respect shows itself in many ways which, incidentally, had better be differentiated from the effects of the love relationship *per se.* Love and respect are separable, even though they often go together. It is possible to respect without loving, even at the self-actualizing level. I am not quite so sure that it is possible to love without respecting, but this too may be a possibility. Many of the characteristics that might be considered aspects or attributes of the love relationship are very frequently seen to be attributes of the respect relationship.

Respect for another person acknowledges him as an independent entity and as a separate and autonomous individual. The self-actualizing person will not casually use another or control him or disregard his wishes. He will allow the respected person a fundamental irreducible dignity, and will not unnecessarily humiliate him. This is true not only for inter-adult relationships but also in a self-actualizing person's relationship to children. It is possible for him, as for practically nobody else in our culture, to treat a child with real respect.

One amusing aspect of this respect relationship between the sexes is that it is very frequently interpreted in just the opposite way, i.e., as a lack of respect. For example, we know well that a good many of the so-called signs of respect for "ladies" are in fact hangovers from a non-respecting past, and possibly even at this time are unconscious representations of a deep unconscious contempt for women. Such cultural habits as standing up when a woman enters the room, giving a lady the chair, helping her with her coat, allowing her to go first through the door, giving her the best of everything and the first choice of everything—these all imply historically and dynamically the opinion that the woman is weak and incapable of taking care of herself, for these all imply protection, as for the weak and incapable. Generally, women who respect themselves strongly tend to dislike these signs of "respect," knowing full well that they may mean just the opposite. Self-actualizing men who tend really and basically to respect and to like women as partners, as equals, as pals, and as full human beings rather than as partial members of the species, are apt to be much more easy and free and familiar and "impolite" in the traditional sense. I have seen this make for trouble, and I have seen self-actualizing men accused of lack of "respect" for women.

8. Love as End-experience; Admiration; Wonder; Awe

The fact that love has many good effects does not mean that it is motivated by those effects or that people fall in love *in order* to achieve them. The love that is found in healthy people is much better described in terms of spontaneous admiration and of the kind of receptive and undemanding awe and enjoyment which we experience when struck by a fine painting. There is too much talk in the literature of rewards and purposes, of reinforcements and gratifications, and not nearly enough of what we may call the "end-experience" (as contrasted with the "means-experience") or "awe-before-the-beautiful."

Admiration and love in my subjects are most of the time *per se* undemanding of rewards and conducive to no purposes, "experienced," in Northrop's Eastern sense [25], concretely and richly, for their own sake, ideographically. [20]

Admiration asks for nothing and gets nothing. It is more passive than active and comes close to simple receiving in the naive-realistic sense. The awed perceiver does little or nothing to the experience; rather it does something to him. He watches and stares with the Innocent Eye, like a child who neither agrees nor disagrees, approves nor disapproves, but who, fascinated by the intrinsic attention-attracting quality of the experience, simply lets it come in and achieve its effects. The experience may be likened to the eager passivity with which we allow ourselves to be tumbled by waves just for the fun that's in it; or perhaps better, to the impersonal interest and awed unprojecting appreciation of the slowly changing sunset. There is little we can inject into a sunset. In this sense we do not project ourselves into the experience or attempt to shape it as we do with the Rorschach. Nor is it a signal or symbol for anything; we have not been rewarded or associated into admiring it. It has nothing to do with milk, or food, or other body needs. In the same way we can enjoy a painting without wanting to own it, a rosebush without wanting to pluck from it, a pretty baby without wanting to kidnap it, a bird without wanting to cage it, and so also can one person admire and enjoy another in a non-doing or non-getting way. Of course awe and admiration lie side by side with other tendencies that *do* involve individuals with each other; it is not the *only* tendency in the picture, but it is definitely part of it, especially in people who are less ego-involved.

Perhaps the most important implication of this observation is that we thereby contradict most theories of love, for most theorists assume that people are *driven* into loving another rather than *attracted* into it. Freud [12] speaks of aim-inhibited sexuality, Reik [27] speaks of aim-inhibited power, and many speak of dissatisfaction with the self forcing us to create a projected hallucination, an unreal (because overestimated) partner.

But it seems clear that healthy people fall in love the way one reacts to one's first appreciative perception of great music—one is awed and overwhelmed by it and loves it. This is so even though there was no prior need to be overwhelmed by great music. Horney in a lecture has defined un-neurotic love in terms of regarding others as *per se,* as ends-in-themselves rather than as means-to-ends. The consequent reaction is to enjoy, to admire, to be delighted, to contemplate and appreciate, rather than to use. St. Bernard said it very aptly: "Love seeks no cause beyond itself and no limit; it is its own fruit, its own enjoyment. I love because I love; I love in order that I may love. . . ." [15]

Similar statements are available in abundance in the theological literature. [6] The effort to differentiate godly love from human love was often based on the assumption that disinterested admiration and altruistic love could be only a superhuman ability and not a natural human one. Of course, we must contradict this; human beings at their best, fully grown, show many *other* characteristics once thought, in an earlier era, to be supernatural prerogatives.

It is my opinion that these phenomena are best understood in the framework of certain theoretical considerations. I have presented these in previous papers. [19–23] In the first place, let us consider the differentiation between deficiency-motivation and growth-motivation (or better, growth-expression). I have suggested that self-actualizers can be defined as people who are no longer motivated by the needs for safety, belongingness, love, status, and self-respect because these needs *have already been satisfied.* Why then should a love-gratified person fall in love? Certainly not for the same reasons that motivate the love-deprived person, who falls in love because he needs and craves love, because he lacks it, and is impelled to make up this pathogenic deficiency.

Self-actualizers have no deficiencies to make up and must now be looked upon as freed for growth, maturation, development, in a word, for the fulfillment and actualization of their highest individual and species nature. What such people do emanates from growth and expresses it without striving. They love because they are loving persons, in the same way that they are kind, honest, natural, i.e., because it is their nature to be so spontaneously, as a strong man is strong without willing to be, as a rose emits perfume, or as a child is childish. Such epiphenomena are as little motivated as is physical growth or psychological maturation.

There is no trying, straining, or striving in the loving of the self-actualizer as there is in the loving of the average person. If we say that it is an aspect of Being as well as of Becoming, those who are familiar with the philosophical literature will understand.

9. Detachment and Individuality

A paradox seems to be created at first sight by the fact that self-actualizing people maintain a degree of individuality, of detachment and autonomy which seems at first glance to be incompatible with the kind of identification and love that I have been describing above. But this is only an apparent paradox. In fact the tendencies existing in the same man to detachment and to need-identification and to profound interrelationships with another person can all co-exist in healthy people. The fact is that self-actualizing people are simultaneously the most individualistic and the most altruistic and social and loving of all human beings. The fact that we have in our culture put these qualities at opposite ends of a single continuum is apparently a mistake that must now be corrected. These qualities go together and the dichotomy is resolved in self-actualizing people.

We find in our subjects a healthy selfishness, a great self-respect, a disinclination to make sacrifices without good reason.

What we see in the love relationship is a fusion of great ability to love and at the same time great respect for the other and great respect for one's self. This shows itself in the fact that these people cannot be said in the ordinary sense of the word to *need* each other as do ordinary lovers. They can be extremely close together and yet go apart quite easily. They do not cling to each other or have hooks or anchors of any kind. One has the definite feeling that they enjoy each other tremendously but would take philosophically a long separation or death. Throughout the most intense and ecstatic love affairs, these people remain themselves and remain ultimately masters of themselves as well, living by their own standards even though enjoying each other intensely.

Obviously, this finding, if confirmed, will necessitate a revision or at least an extension in the definition of ideal or healthy love in our culture. We have customarily defined it in terms of a complete merging of egos and a loss of separateness, a giving up of individuality rather than a strengthening of it. While this is true, the fact appears to be at this moment that the individuality is strengthened, that the ego is in one sense merged with another, but yet in another sense remains separate and strong as always. The two tendencies, to transcend individuality and to sharpen and strengthen it, must be seen as partners and not as contradictories.

10. The Greater Taste and Perceptiveness of Healthy Lovers

One of the most striking superiorities reported of self-actualizing people is their exceptional perceptiveness. They can perceive truth and reality far more efficiently than the average run of people, whether it is structured or unstructured, personal or non-personal.

This acuity manifests itself in the area of love-relations primarily in an excellent taste (or perceptiveness) in sexual and love partners. The close friends, husbands, and wives of our subjects make a far finer group of human beings than random sampling would dictate.

This is not to say that *all* the observed marriages and choices of sexual partner were at the self-actualizing level. Several mistakes can be reported, and although they can be to some extent explained away, they testify to the fact that our subjects are not perfect or omniscient. They have their vanities and their own special weaknesses. For example, at least one man of those I studied married more out of pity than out of equalitarian love. One married a woman much younger than himself, in the face of the inevitable problems. A measured statement would then stress that their taste in mates, while much better than average, is by no means perfect.

But even this is enough to contradict the generally held belief that love is blind or, in the more sophisticated versions of this mistake, that the lover necessarily overestimates his partner. It is quite clear that, though this probably is true for average people, it need not be true for healthy individuals. Indeed, there are even some indications that the perceptions of healthy people are *more* efficient, more acute when in love than when not. Love may make it possible to see qualities in the loved person of which others are completely oblivious.[5] It is easy enough to make this mistake because healthy people can fall in love with people whom others would not love for very definite "faults." However, this love is not blind to the faults; it simply overlooks these perceived faults, or else does not regard them as shortcomings. Thus physical imperfections, as well as economic, educational, and social shortcomings, are far less important to healthy people than are character defects. As a consequence, it is easily possible for self-actualizing people to fall deeply in love with homely partners. This is called blindness by others, but it might much better be called good taste.

I have had the opportunity of watching the development of this "good taste" in several realtively healthy young college men and women. The more mature they became, the less attracted they were by such characteristics as "handsome," "good-looking," "good dancer," "nice breasts," "physically strong," "tall," "handsome body," "good necker," and the more they spoke of compatibility, goodness, decency, good companionship, considerateness. In a few cases, it could actually be seen that they fell in love with individuals with characteristics considered specifically distasteful a few years before, e.g., hair on the body, too fat, not smart enough. In one young man, I have seen the number of potential sweethearts grow fewer year by year until, from being attracted to practically any one female, and with exclusions being solely on a physical basis (too fat, too tall), he could think of making love with only two girls from among all that he knew. These were now spoken of in characterological rather than physical terms.

I think research will show that this is more characteristic of increasing health than simply of increasing age.

Two other common theories are contradicted by our data. One is that opposites attract, and the other is that like marries like (homog-

---

[5] Oswald Schwarz, *The Psychology of Sex*, (Harmondsworth, Middlesex: Penguin Books, 1951): "It cannot be emphasized strongly enough that this miraculous capacity which love bestows on the lovers consists in the power to discover in the object of love virtues which it actually possesses but which are invisible to the uninspired; they are not invented by the lover, who decorates the beloved with illusory values: love is no self-deception." (pp. 100–101) "No doubt there is a strong emotional element in it but essentially love is a cognitive act, indeed the only way to grasp the innermost core of personality." (p. 20)

amy). The facts of the matter are that in healthy people homogamy is the rule with respect to such character traits as honesty, sincerity, kindliness, and courage. In the more external and superficial characteristics, e.g., income, class status, education, religion, national background, appearance, the extent of homogamy seems to be significantly less than in average people. Self-actualizing people are not threatened by differences nor by strangeness. Indeed, they are rather intrigued than otherwise. They need familiar accents, clothes, food, customs, and ceremonies much less than do average people. [22]

As for opposites attracting, this is true for my subjects to the extent that I have seen honest admiration for skills and talents which they themselves do not possess. Such superiorities make a potential partner *more* rather than less attractive to my subjects, whether in man or in woman.

Finally, I wish to call attention to another implication of considerable importance. The last few pages amount to a resolution or denial of the age-old dichotomy between impulse and reason, between "head" and "heart." The people with whom my subjects fall in love are soundly selected by *either* cognitive or conative criteria. That is, they are *intuitively, sexually, impulsively* attracted to people who are right for them by cold, intellectual, clinical calculation. Their appetites agree with their judgments, and are synergetic rather than antagonistic, as they very frequently are in average people and neurotics.

This reminds us of Sorokin's efforts [32] to demonstrate that the true, the good, and the beautiful are positively interrelated. Our data seem to confirm Sorokin, but *only for healthy people*. With respect to neurotic people, we must remain circumspect on this question.

11. The Resolution of Dichotomies in Self-actualization

I cannot resist the temptation to underscore a theoretical conclusion to which I have come from the study of self-actualizing people. At several points in this paper—and in other papers as well—it was concluded that what had been considered polarities or dichotomies were so *only in unhealthy people*. This was so for selfishness-unselfishness, reason-instinct (or cognition-conation), individualism-social mindedness, animality-"soulfulness," kindness-ruthlessness, concrete-abstract, acceptance-rebellion, self-society, adjustment-maladjustment, detachment from others-identification with others, childlikeness-maturity, serious-humorous, democratic-aristocratic, moral-amoral, classical-romantic, Apollonian-Dionysian, introverted-extroverted, intense-casual, conventional-unconventional, mystic-realistic, active-passive, masculine-feminine, lust-love, and Eros-Agape.

Fully matured people seem to be so different from average citizens in *kind* as well as in degree that I have come to suspect that the two very different kinds of people will generate two very different psychologies. The psychology that we now teach, being based upon the study of crippled, immature, and unhealthy specimens, must be suspected of not being large enough to encompass healthy, fully grown specimens. The cripple-psychology, which is all we now have, must be integrated with, imbedded in, and encompassed by a larger, more inclusive, more universal science of psychology. Such a science must be based upon the study of healthy self-actualizing people.

Bibliography

1. ANGYAL, A., *Foundations For a Science of Personality.* New York: Commonwealth Fund, 1941.

2. ANSBACHER, H., and ROWENA eds., Alfred Adler, *Individual Psychology.* New York: Basic Books, 1956.

3. ASHLEY MONTAGU, M. F., *On Being Human.* New York: H. Schuman, 1950.

4. BALINT, M., "On Genital Love," *International Journal of Psychoanalysis,* 29 (1948), 34–40.

5. BERGLER, E., *Neurotic Counterfeit-Sex.* New York: Grune and Stratton, 1951.

6. D'ARCY, *The Mind and Heart of Love.* New York: Holt, 1947.

7. DeFOREST, I., "Love and Anger, the Two Activating Forces in Psychoanalytic Therapy," *Psychiatry,* 7 (1944), 15–29.

8. DREIKURS, R., *The Challenge of Marriage.* New York: Duell, Sloan and Pearce, 1946.

9. FREUD, S., *Collected Papers,* Vol. II. London: Hogarth, 1925.

10. FREUD, S., *General Introduction to Psychoanalysis.* New York: Garden City Publishing Co., 1920.

11. FREUD, S., *Contributions to the Psychology of Love,* Papers XI, XII, XIII in *Collected Papers,* Vol. 4, 192–235. London: Hogarth, 1925.

12. FREUD, S., *Civilization and Its Discontents.* New York: Cape and Smith, 1930.

13. FROMM, E., *Escape From Freedom.* New York: Farrar and Rinehart, 1941.

14. FROMM, E., *Man For Himself.* New York: Rinehart, 1947.

15. HUXLEY, A., *The Perennial Philosophy.* New York: Harper, 1945.

16. IOVETZ-TERESHCHENKO, N., *Friendship—Love in Adolescence.* London: George Allen and Unwin, 1936.

17. JEKELS, L., and E. BERGLER, "Transference and Love," *Psychoanalytic Quarterly,* 18 (1949), 325–50.

18. LEVY, D. M., "The Deprived and Indulged Forms of Psychopathic Personality," *American Journal of Orthopsychiatry,* 21 (1951), 250–54.

19. MASLOW, A. H., "Some Theoretical Consequences of Basic Need-Gratification," *Journal of Personality,* 16 (1948), 402–16.

20. MASLOW, A. H., "The Expressive Component of Behavior," *Psychological Review,* 56 (1949), 261–72.

21. MASLOW, A. H., "Resistance to Acculturation," *Journal of Social Issues,* 7 (1951), 4, 26–29.

22. MASLOW, A. H., "Self-Actualizing People; a Study in Psychological Health," *Personality,* 1 (1950), 11–34 (Symposium No. 1 on Values).

23. MASLOW, A. H., "The Instinctoid Nature of Basic Needs," *Journal of Personality,* 1952.

24. MENNINGER, K., *Love against Hate.* London: Kegan Paul, Trench, Trubner, 1935.

25. NORTHROP, F. S. C., *The Meeting of East and West.* New York: Macmillan, 1946.

26. OVERSTREET, H., *The Mature Mind.* New York: W. W. Norton, 1949.

27. REIK, T., *The Psychology of Sex Relations.* New York: Farrar and Rinehart, 1945.

28. ROGERS, C., *Client-Centered Therapy.* New York: Houghton Mifflin, 1951.

29. SAUL, L., *Emotional Maturity.* Philadelphia: Lippincott, 1947.

30. SCHLICK, M., *Problems of Ethics.* New York: Prentice-Hall, 1939.

31. SCHWARZ, O., *The Psychology of Sex.* London: Penguin Books, 1951.

32. SOROKIN, P., ed., *Explorations in Altruistic Love and Behavior.* Boston: Beacon Press, 1950.

33. SUTTIE, I., *The Origins of Love and Hate.* New York: Julian Press, 1952.

34. SYMONDS, P., *The Dynamics of Human Adjustment.* New York: Appleton-Century-Crofts, 1946.

35. WEXBERG, E., *The Psychology of Sex.* New York: Farrar and Rinehart, 1931.

ℛOLLO ℳAY

A Preface to Love

Rollo May here gives us a down-to-earth, honest, and unsentimental statement of the meaning of love, what it presupposes, how little there is of it in our world, and the hypocrisy of much that passes for the genuine article. He points out that tenderness goes along with strength; that it is really the weak who have to hide behind a barrier of toughness. Wherever there is a taboo on tenderness we may suspect an unwillingness or an inability to engage in the labor of being involved.

. . . To be capable of giving and receiving mature love is as sound a criterion as we have for the fulfilled personality. But by that very token it is a goal gained only in proportion to how much one has fulfilled the prior condition of becoming a person in one's own right. . . .

In the first place it should be noted that love is actually a relatively rare phenomenon in our society. As everyone knows, there are a million and one kinds of relationships which are *called* love: we do not need to list all of the confusions of "love" with sentimental impulses and every kind of oedipal and "back to mother's arms" motifs as they appear in the romantic songs and the movies. No word is used with more meanings than this term, most of the meanings being dishonest in that they cover up the real underlying motives in the relationship. But there are many other quite sound and honest relationships called love—such as parental care for children and vice versa, or sexual passion, or the sharing of loneliness; and again the startling reality often discovered when one looks underneath the surface of the individuals' lives in our lonely and conformist society, is how little the component of love is actually involved even in these relationships.

Most human relationships, of course, spring from a mixture of

"A Preface to Love" (editor's title). From Rollo May, Ph.D., *Man's Search for Himself* (New York: W. W. Norton & Company, Inc., 1953), pp. 238–46. Copyright 1953 by W. W. Norton & Company, Inc. Reprinted by permission of W. W. Norton & Company, Inc., and Souvenir Press.

motives and include a combination of different feelings. Sexual love in its mature form between a man and woman is generally a blend of two emotions. One is "eros"—the sexual drive toward the other, which is part of the individual's need to fulfill himself. Two and a half millennia ago Plato pictured "eros" as the drive of each individual to unite with the complement to himself—the drive to find the other half of the original "androgyne," the mythological being who was both man and woman. The other element in mature love between man and woman is the affirmation of the value and worth of the other person, which we include in our definition of love given below.

But granted the blending of motives and emotions, and granted that love is not a simple topic, the most important thing at the outset is to call our emotions by their right names. And the most constructive place to begin learning how to love is to see how we fail to love. We shall have made a start, at least, when we recognize our situation as that of the young man in Auden's *The Age of Anxiety:*

> So, learning to love, at length he is taught
> To know he does not.

Our society is, as we have seen, the heir of four centuries of competitive individualism, with power over others as a dominant motivation; and our particular generation is the heir of a good deal of anxiety, isolation and personal emptiness. These are scarcely good preparations for learning how to love.

When we look at the topic on the level of national relations, we come to similar conclusions. It is easy enough to slide into the comforting sentiment, "Love will solve all." To be sure, it is obvious that this distraught world's political and social problems cry out for the attitudes of empathy, imaginative concern, love for the neighbor and "the stranger." Elsewhere I have pointed out that what our society lacks is the experience of community, based on socially valuable work and love—and lacking community we fall into its neurotic substitute, the "neurosis of collectivism." [1] But it is not helpful to tell people, *ipso facto,* that they should love. This only promotes hypocrisy and sham, of which we have a good deal too much in the area of love already. Sham and hypocrisy are greater deterrents to learning to love than is outright hostility, for at least the latter may be honest and can then be worked with. Simply the proclaiming of the point that the world's hostilities and hatreds would be overcome if only people could love invites more

[1] See Rollo May, *The Meaning of Anxiety* (New York: Ronald Press, 1950), Chapter 5.

hypocrisy; and furthermore, we have learned in our dealings with Russia how crucial it is to lead from strength, and to meet authoritarian sadism directly and realistically. Certainly every new act in international relations which affirms the values and needs of other nations and groups, as did the Marshall Plan, should be welcomed with rejoicing. At least we are learning at long last that we must affirm other nations' existence for our own sheer survival. But though such lessons are great gains, we cannot thereby conclude that occasional actions of this kind are a proof that we have learned—on the political level—to love. So, again, we shall make our most useful contribution to a world in dire need of concern for the neighbor and stranger if we begin by trying to make ourselves as individuals able to love. Lewis Mumford has remarked, "As with peace, those who call for love loudest often express it least. To make ourselves capable of loving, and ready to receive love, is the paramount problem of integration; indeed the key to salvation."

So great is the confusion about love in our day that it is even difficult to find [people] agreed upon definitions of what love is. We define love as *a delight in the presence of the other person and an affirming of his value and development as much as one's own.* Thus there are always two elements to love—that of the worth and good of the other person, and that of one's own joy and happiness in the relation with him.

The capacity to love presupposes self-awareness, because love requires the ability to have empathy with the other person, to appreciate and affirm his potentialities. Love also presupposes freedom; certainly love which is not freely given is not love. To "love" someone because you are not free to love someone else, or because you happen by the accident of birth to be in some family relation to him, is not to love. Furthermore, if one "loves" because one cannot do without the other, love is not given by choice; for one could not choose not to love. The hallmark of such unfree "love" is that it does not discriminate: it does not distinguish the "loved" person's qualities or his being from the next person's. In such a relation you are not really "seen" by the one who purports to love you—you might just as well be someone else. Neither the one who loves nor the loved one act as *persons* in such relationships; the former is not a subject operating with some freedom, and the latter is significant chiefly as an object to be clung to.

There are all kinds of dependence which in our society—having so many anxious, lonely and empty persons in it—masquerade as love. They vary from different forms of mutual aid or reciprocal satisfaction of desires (which may be quite sound if called by their right names), through the various "business" forms of personal relationships to clear parasitical masochism. It not infrequently happens that two persons, feeling solitary and empty by themselves, relate to each other in a kind of unspoken bargain to keep each other from suffering loneliness. Matthew Arnold described this beautifully in *Dover Beach:*

> Ah, love, let us be true
> To one another! for the world, which seems
> To lie before us like a land of dreams,
> So various, so beautiful, so new,
> Hath really neither joy, nor love, nor light,
> Nor certitude, nor peace, nor help for pain;
> And we are here as on a darkling plain. . . .

But when "love" is engaged in for the purpose of vanquishing loneliness, it accomplishes its purpose only at the price of increased emptiness for both persons.

Love, as we have said, is generally confused with dependence: but in point of fact, you can love only in proportion to your capacity for independence. Harry Stack Sullivan has made the startling statement that a child cannot learn "to love anybody before he is pre-adolescent. You can get him to sound like it, to act so you can believe it. But there is no real basis and if you stress it you get queer results, many of which become neuroses." [2] That is to say, until this age the capacity for awareness and affirmation of other persons has not matured enough for love. As an infant and child he is quite normally dependent on his parents, and he may in fact be very fond of them, like to be with them, and so forth. Let parents and children frankly enjoy the happiness such a relationship makes possible. But it is very healthy and relieving for parents, in the respect of reducing their need to play god and their tendency to arrogate to themselves complete importance in nature's scheme for the child's life, to note how much more spontaneous warmth and "care" the child shows in dealing with his teddy bear or doll or, later on, his real dog than he shows in his relations with human beings. The bear or doll makes no demands on him; he can project into them all he likes, and he does not have to force himself beyond his degree of maturity to empathize with their needs. The live dog is an intermediate step between the inanimate objects and human beings. Each step—from dependence, through dependability to interdependence—represents the developmental stage of the child's maturing capacity for love.

---

[2] In Dr. Sullivan's paper in *Culture and Personality*, ed. Sargent and Smith (New York: Viking Fund, 1949), p. 194.

One of the chief things which keeps us from learning to love in our society, as Erich Fromm and others have pointed out, is our "marketplace orientation." We use love for buying and selling. One illustration of this is in the fact that many parents expect that the child love them as a repayment for their taking care of him. To be sure, a child will learn to pretend to certain acts of love if the parents insist on it; but sooner or later it turns out that a love demanded as a payment is no love at all. Such love is a "house built upon sand" and often collapses with a crash when the children have grown into young adulthood. For why does the fact that the parent has supported or protected a child, sent him to camp and later to college, have anything necessarily to do with his loving the parent? It could as logically be expected that the son should love the city traffic policeman on the corner who protects him from trucks or the army mess sergeant who gets him his food when he is in the army.

A deeper form of this demand is that the child should love the parent because the parent has sacrificed for him. But sacrifice may be simply another form of bargaining and may have nothing to do in motivation with an affirmation of the other's values and development.

We receive love—from our children as well as others—not in proportion to our demands or sacrifices or needs, but roughly in proportion to our own capacity to love. And our capacity to love depends, in turn, upon our prior capacity to be persons in our own right. To love means, essentially, to give; and to give requires a maturity of self-feeling. Love is shown in the statement of Spinoza's [quoted in the original printing], that truly loving God does not involve a demand for love in return. It is the attitude referred to by the artist Joseph Binder: "To produce art requires that the artist be able to love—that is to give without thought of being rewarded."

We are not talking about love as a "giving *up*" or self-abnegation. One gives only if he has something to give, only if he has a basis of strength within himself from which to give. It is most unfortunate in our society that we have had to try to purify love from aggression and competitive triumph by identifying it with weakness. Indeed, this inoculation has been so much of a success that the common prejudice is that the weaker people are, the more they love; and that the strong man does not *need* to love! No wonder tenderness, that yeast without which love is as soggy and heavy as unrisen bread, has been generally scorned, and often separated out of the love experience.

What was forgotten was that tenderness goes along with strength: one can be gentle as he is strong; otherwise tenderness and gentleness are masquerades for clinging. The Latin origin of our words is nearer the truth—"virtue," of which love is certainly one, comes from the root *vir*, "man" (here in the sense of masculine strength), from which the word "virility" is also derived.

Some readers may be questioning, "But does one not *lose* himself in love?" To be sure, in love as in creative consciousness, it is true that one is merged with the other. But this should not be called "losing one's self"; again like creative consciousness, it is the highest level of fulfillment of one's self. When sex is an expression of love, for example, the emotion experienced at the moment of orgasm is not hostility or triumph, but *union* with the other person. The poets are not lying to us when they sing of the ecstasy in love. As in creative ecstasy, it is that moment of self-realization when one temporarily overleaps the barrier between one identity and another. It is a giving of one's self and a finding of one's self at once. Such ecstasy represents the fullest interdependence in human relations; and the same paradox applies as in creative consciousness—one can merge one's self in ecstasy only as one has gained the prior capacity to stand alone, to be a person in one's own right.

We do not mean this discussion to be a counsel of perfection. Nor is it meant to rule out or depreciate all of the other kinds of positive relationships, such as friendship (which may also be an important aspect of parent-child relations), various degrees of interchange of human warmth and understanding, the sharing of sexual pleasure and passion, and so on. Let us not fall into the error so common in our society of making love in its ideal sense all-important, so that one has only the alternatives of admitting he has never found the "pearl of great price" or resorting to hypocrisy in trying to persuade himself that all of the emotions he does feel are "love." We can only repeat: we propose calling the emotions by their right names. Learning to love will proceed most soundly if we cease trying to persuade ourselves that to love is easy, and if we are realistic enough to abandon the illusory masquerades for love in a society which is always talking about love but has so little of it.

WILLIAM J. GOODE

The Theoretical Importance
of Love*

In this contribution Professor Goode questions the general anthropological assumption that love as it is known in civilized societies is unknown among nonliterate people. That love, here defined as a strong emotional attachment with at least the components of sex desire and tenderness, exists in all societies, cannot be doubted. But love is a passion that can cause much disruption. Every society has instituted controls on it. Here Goode considers the kinds of controls that different societies have devised to check the potential social disruption caused by love.

As will be perceived in the development of his theme, the apparent absence of love in many less "civilized" societies is due not to the absence of the possibilities for its development but to their deliberate early arrest, chiefly by parents and others of the parental generation. Professor Goode shows that such controls are exercised in all societies, particularly along religious, caste, class and racial lines in the more advanced societies.

Because love often determines the intensity of an attraction[1] toward or away from an intimate relationship with another person, it can become one element in a decision or action.[2] Nevertheless, serious sociological

"The Theoretical Importance of Love" by William J. Goode. From *American Sociological Review*, 24, no. 1, February 1959, 38–47. Reprinted by permission of the author and the American Sociological Association.

* This paper was completed under a grant (No. M-2526-S) by the National Institute of Mental Health.

[1] On the psychological level, the motivational power of both love and sex is intensified by this curious fact (which I have not seen remarked on elsewhere): Love is the most projective of emotions, as sex is the most projective of drives; only with great difficulty can the attracted person believe that the object of his love or passion does not and will not reciprocate the feeling at all. Thus, the person may carry his action quite far, before accepting a rejection as genuine.

[2] I have treated decision analysis extensively in an unpublished paper by that title.

attention has only infrequently been given to love. Moreover, analyses of love generally have been confined to mate choice in the Western World, while the structural importance of love has been for the most part ignored. The present paper views love in a broad perspective, focusing on the structural patterns by which societies keep in check the potentially disruptive effect of love relationships on mate choice and stratification systems.

Types of Literature on Love

For obvious reasons, the printed material on love is immense. For our present purposes, it may be classified as follows:

1. Poetic, humanistic, literary, erotic, pornographic: By far the largest body of all literature on love views it as a sweeping experience. The poet arouses our sympathy and empathy. The essayist enjoys, and asks the reader to enjoy, the interplay of people in love. The storyteller—Boccaccio, Chaucer, Dante—pulls back the curtain of human souls and lets the reader watch the intimate lives of others caught in an emotion we all know. Others—Vatsyayana, Ovid, William IX Count of Poitiers and Duke of Aquitaine, Marie de France, Andreas Capellanus—have written how-to-do-it books, that is, how to conduct oneself in love relations, to persuade others to succumb to one's love wishes, or to excite and satisfy one's sex partner.[3]

2. Marital counseling: Many modern sociologists have commented on the importance of romantic love in America and its lesser importance in other societies, and have disparaged it as a poor basis for marriage, or as immaturity. Perhaps the best known ·of these arguments are those of Ernest R. Mowrer, Ernest W. Burgess, Mabel A. Elliott, Andrew G. Truxal, Francis E. Merrill, and Ernest R. Groves.[4]

---

[3] Vatsyayana, *The Kama Sutra* (Delhi: Rajkamal, 1948); Ovid, "The Loves," and "Remedies of Love," in *The Art of Love* (Cambridge, Mass.: Harvard University Press, 1939); Andreas Capellanus, *The Art of Courtly Love*, transl. John J. Parry (New York: Columbia University press, 1941); Paul Tuffrau, ed. *Marie de France: Les Lais de Marie de France* (Paris: L'edition d'art, 1925); see also Julian Harris, *Marie de France* (New York: Institute of French Studies, 1930), esp. Chapter 3. All authors but the first *also* had the goal of writing literature.

[4] Ernest R. Mowrer, *Family Disorganization* (Chicago: The University of Chicago Press, 1927), pp. 158–65; Ernest W. Burgess and Harvey J. Locke, *The Family* (New York: American Book, 1953), pp. 436–37; Mabel A. Elliott and Francis E. Merrill, *Social Disorganization* (New York: Harper, 1950), pp. 366–84; Andrew G. Truxal and Francis E. Merrill, *The Family in American Culture* (New York: Prentice-Hall, 1947), pp. 120–24, 507–509; Ernest R. Groves and Gladys Hoagland Groves, *The Contemporary American Family* (New York: Lippincott, 1947), pp. 321–24.

The antithesis of romantic love, in such analyses, is "conjugal" love; the love between a settled, domestic couple.

A few sociologists, remaining within this same evaluative context, have instead claimed that love also has salutary effects in our society. Thus, for example, William L. Kolb[5] has tried to demonstrate that the marital counselors who attack romantic love are really attacking some fundamental values of our larger society, such as individualism, freedom, and personality growth. Beigel[6] has argued that if the female is sexually repressed, only the psychotherapist or love can help her overcome her inhibitions. He claims further that one influence of love in our society is that it extenuates illicit sexual relations; he goes on to assert: "Seen in proper perspective, [love] has not only done no harm as a prerequisite to marriage, but it has mitigated the impact that a too-fast-moving and unorganized conversion to new socio-economic constellations has had upon our whole culture and it has saved monogamous marriage from complete disorganization."

In addition, there is widespread comment among marriage analysts, that in a rootless society, with few common bases for companionship, romantic love holds a couple together long enough to allow them to begin marriage. That is, it functions to attract people powerfully together, and to hold them through the difficult first months of the marriage, when their different backgrounds would otherwise make an adjustment troublesome.

3. Although the writers cited above concede the structural importance of love implicitly, since they are arguing that it is either harmful or helpful to various values and goals of our society, a third group has given explicit if unsystematic attention to its structural importance. Here, most of the available propositions point to the functions of love, but a few deal with the conditions under which love relationships occur. They include:

- An implicit or assumed descriptive proposition is that love as a common prelude to and basis of marriage is rare, perhaps to be found as a pattern only in the United States.

- Most explanations of the conditions which create love are psychological, stemming from Freud's notion that love is "aim-inhibited sex." [7] This idea is expressed, for example, by Waller, who says that love is an idealized passion which develops from the frustration of sex.[8] This proposition,

[5] William L. Kolb, "Sociologically Established Norms and Democratic Values," *Social Forces*, 26 (May, 1948), 451–56.

[6] Hugo G. Beigel, "Romantic Love," *American Sociological Review*, 16 (June, 1951), 326–34.

[7] Sigmund Freud, *Group Psychology and the Analysis of the Ego* (London: Hogarth, 1922), p. 72.

[8] Willard Waller, *The Family* (New York: Dryden, 1938), pp. 189–92.

although rather crudely stated and incorrect as a general explanation, is widely accepted.

- Of course, a predisposition to love is created by the socialization experience. Thus some textbooks on the family devote extended discussion to the ways in which our society socializes for love. The child, for example, is told that he or she will grow up to fall in love with someone, and early attempts are made to pair the child with children of the opposite sex. There is much joshing of children about falling in love; myths and stories about love and courtship are heard by children; and so on.

- A further proposition (the source of which I have not been able to locate) is that, in a society in which a very close attachment between parent and child prevails, a love complex is necessary in order to motivate the child to free him from his attachment to his parents.

- Love is also described as one final or crystallizing element in the decision to marry, which is otherwise structured by factors such as class, ethnic origin, religion, education, and residence.

- Parsons has suggested three factors which "underlie the prominence of the romantic context in our culture": (a) the youth culture frees the individual from family attachments, thus permitting him to fall in love; (b) love is a substitute for the interlocking of kinship roles found in other societies, and thus motivates the individual to conform to proper marital role behavior; and (c) the structural isolation of the family so frees the married partners' affective inclinations that they are able to love one another.[9]

- Robert F. Winch has developed a theory of "complementary needs" which essentially states that the underlying dynamic in the process of falling in love is an interaction between (a) the perceived psychological attributes of one individual and (b) the complementary psychological attributes of the person falling in love, such that the needs of the latter are felt to be met by the perceived attributes of the former and *vice versa*. These needs are derived from Murray's list of personality characteristics. Winch thus does not attempt to solve the problem of why our society has a love complex, but how it is that specific individuals fall in love with each other rather than with someone else.[10]

- Winch and others have also analyzed the effect of love upon various institutions or social patterns: Love themes are prominently displayed in the media of entertainment and communication, in consumption patterns, and so on.[11]

4. Finally, there is the cross-cultural work of anthropologists, who in the main have ignored love as a factor of importance in kinship patterns. The implicit understanding seems to be that love as a pattern

[9] Talcott Parsons, *Essays in Sociological Theory* (Glencoe, Ill.: Free Press, 1949), pp. 187–89.
[10] Robert F. Winch, *Mate Selection* (New York: Harper, 1958).
[11] See, e.g., Robert F. Winch, *The Modern Family* (New York: Holt, 1952), Chapter 14.

is found only in the United States, although of course individual cases of love are sometimes recorded. The term "love" is practically never found in indexes of anthropological monographs on specific societies or in general anthropology textbooks. It is perhaps not an exaggeration to say that Lowie's comment of a generation ago would still be accepted by a substantial number of anthropologists:

But of love among savages? . . . Passion, of course, is taken for granted; affection, which many travelers vouch for, might be conceded; but Love? Well, the romantic sentiment occurs in simpler conditions, as with us—in fiction. . . . So Love exists for the savage as it does for ourselves—in adolescence, in fiction, among the poetically minded.[12]

A still more skeptical opinion is Linton's scathing sneer:

All societies recognize that there are occasional violent, emotional attachments between persons of opposite sex, but our present American culture is practically the only one which has attempted to capitalize these, and make them the basis for marriage. . . . The hero of the modern American movie is always a romantic lover, just as the hero of the old Arab epic is always an epileptic. A cynic may suspect that in any ordinary population the percentage of individuals with a capacity for romantic love of the Hollywood type was about as large as that of persons able to throw genuine epileptic fits.[13]

In Murdock's book on kinship and marriage, there is almost no mention, if any, of love.[14] Should we therefore conclude that, cross-culturally, love is not important, and thus cannot be of great importance structurally? If there is only one significant case, perhaps it is safe to view love as generally unimportant in social structure and to concentrate rather on the nature and functions of romantic love within the Western societies in which love is obviously prevalent. As brought out below, however, many anthropologists have in fact described love *patterns*. And one of them, Max Gluckman,[15] has recently subsumed a wide range of observations under the broad principle that love relationships between husband and wife estrange the couple from their kin, who therefore try in various ways to undermine that love. This principle is applicable to many more societies (for example, China and India) than Gluckman himself discusses.

---

[12] Robert H. Lowie, "Sex and Marriage," in John F. McDermott, ed., *The Sex Problem in Modern Society* (New York: Modern Library, 1931), p. 146.

[13] Ralph Linton, *The Study of Man* (New York: Appleton-Century, 1936), p. 175.

[14] George Peter Murdock, *Social Structure* (New York: Macmillan, 1949).

[15] Max Gluckman, *Custom and Conflict in Africa* (Oxford: Basil Blackwell, 1955), Chapter 3.

The Problem and Its Conceptual Clarification

The preceding propositions (except those denying that love is distributed widely) can be grouped under two main questions: What are the consequences of romantic love in the United States? How is the emotion of love aroused or created in our society? The present paper deals with the first question. For theoretical purposes both questions must be reformulated, however, since they implicitly refer only to our peculiar system of romantic love. Thus: (1) In what ways do various love patterns fit into the social structure, especially into the systems of mate choice and stratification? (2) What are the structural conditions under which a range of love patterns occurs in various societies? These are overlapping questions, but their starting point and assumptions are different. The first assumes that love relationships are a universal psychosocial possibility, and that different social systems make different adjustments to their potential disruptiveness. The second does not take love for granted, and supposes rather that such relationships will be rare unless certain structural factors are present. Since in both cases the analysis need not depend upon the correctness of the assumption, the problem may be chosen arbitrarily. Let us begin with the first.[16]

We face at once the problem of defining "love." Here, love is defined as a strong emotional attachment, a cathexis, between adolescents or adults of opposite sexes, with at least the components of sex desire and tenderness. Verbal definitions of this emotional relationship are notoriously open to attack; this one is no more likely to satisfy critics than others. Agreement is made difficult by value judgments: one critic would exclude anything but "true" love, another casts out "infatuation," another objects to "puppy love," while others would separate sex desire from love because sex presumably is degrading. Nevertheless, most of us have had the experience of love, just as we have been greedy, or melancholy, or moved by hate (defining "true" hate seems not to be a problem). The experience can be referred to without great ambiguity, and a refined measure of various degrees of intensity or purity of love is unnecessary for the aims of the present analysis.

Since love may be related in diverse ways to the social structure, it is necessary to forego the dichotomy of "romantic love—no romantic love" in favor of a continuum or range between polar types. At one pole, a strong love attraction is socially viewed as a laughable or tragic

---

[16] I hope to deal with the second problem in another paper.

aberration; at the other, it is mildly shameful to marry without being in love with one's intended spouse. This is a gradation from negative sanction to positive approval, ranging at the same time from low or almost nonexistent institutionalization of love to high institutionalization.

The urban middle classes of contemporary Western society, especially in the United States, are found toward the latter pole. Japan and China, in spite of the important movement toward European patterns, fall toward the pole of low institutionalization. Village and urban India is farther toward the center, for there the ideal relationship has been one which at least generated love after marriage, and sometimes after betrothal, in contrast with the mere respect owed between Japanese and Chinese spouses.[17] Greece after Alexander, Rome of the Empire, and perhaps the later period of the Roman Republic as well, are near the center, but somewhat toward the pole of institutionalization, for love matches appear to have increased in frequency—a trend denounced by moralists.[18]

This conceptual continuum helps to clarify our problem and to interpret the propositions reviewed above. Thus it may be noted, first, that individual love relationships may occur even in societies in which love is viewed as irrelevant to mate choice and excluded from the decision to marry. As Linton conceded, some violent love attachments may be found in any society. In our own, the Song of Solomon, Jacob's love of Rachel, and Michal's love for David are classic tales. The Mahabharata, the great Indian epic, includes love themes. Romantic love appears early in Japanese literature, and the use of Mt. Fuji as a locale for the suicide of star-crossed lovers is not a myth invented by editors of tabloids. There is the familiar tragic Chinese story to be found on the traditional "willowplate," with its lovers transformed into doves. And so it goes—individual love relationships seem to occur everywhere. But this fact does not change the position of a society on the continuum.

Second, reading both Linton's and Lowie's comments in this new

[17] Tribal India, of course, is too heterogeneous to place in any one position on such a continuum. The question would have to be answered for each tribe. Obviously it is of less importance here whether China and Japan, in recent decades, have moved "two points over" toward the opposite pole of high approval of love relationships as a basis for marriage than that both systems as classically described viewed love as generally a tragedy; and love was supposed to be irrelevant to marriage, i.e., noninstitutionalized. The continuum permits us to place a system at some position, once we have the descriptive data.

[18] See Ludwig Friedländer, *Roman Life and Manners under the Early Empire*, 7th ed., transl. A. Magnus, (New York: Dutton, 1908), Vol. I, Chapter 5, "The Position of Women."

conceptual context reduces their theoretical importance, for they are both merely saying that people do not *live by* the romantic complex, here or anywhere else. Some few couples in love will brave social pressures, physical dangers, or the gods themselves, but nowhere is this usual. Violent, self-sufficient love is not common anywhere. In this respect, of course, the U.S. is not set apart from other systems.

Third, we can separate a *love pattern* from the romantic love *complex*. Under the former, love is a permissible, expected prelude to marriage, and a usual element of courtship—thus, at about the center of the continuum, but toward the pole of institutionalization. The romantic love complex (one pole of the continuum) includes, in addition, an ideological prescription that falling in love is a highly desirable basis of courtship and marriage; love is strongly institutionalized.[19] In contemporary United States, many individuals would even claim that entering marriage without being in love requires some such rationalization as asserting that one is too old for such romances or that one must "think of practical matters like money." To be sure, both anthropologists and sociologists often exaggerate the American commitment to romance;[20] nevertheless, a behavioral and value complex of this type is found here.

But this complex is rare. Perhaps only the following cultures possess the romantic love value complex: modern urban United States, Northwestern Europe, Polynesia, and the European nobility of the eleventh and twelfth centuries.[21] Certainly, it is to be found in no other major civilization. On the other hand, the *love pattern*, which views love as a basis for the final decision to marry, may be relatively common.

[19] For a discussion of the relation between behavior patterns and the process of institutionalization, see my *After Divorce* (Glencoe, Ill.: Free Press, 1956), Chapter 15.

[20] See Ernest W. Burgess and Paul W. Wallin, *Engagement and Marriage* (New York: Lippincott, 1953), Chapter 7 for the extent to which even the engaged are not blind to the defects of their beloveds. No one has ascertained the degree to which various age and sex groups in our society actually believe in some form of the ideology.

Similarly, Margaret Mead in *Coming of Age in Samoa* (New York: Modern Library, 1953), rates Manu'an love as shallow, and though these Samoans give much attention to love-making, she asserts that they laughed with incredulous contempt at Romeo and Juliet (pp. 155–56). Though the individual sufferer showed jealousy and anger, the Manu'ans believed that a new love would quickly cure a betrayed lover (pp. 105–108). It is possible that Mead failed to understand the shallowness of love in our own society: Romantic love is, "in our civilization, inextricably bound up with ideas of monogamy, exclusiveness, jealousy, and undeviating fidelity" (p. 105). But these are *ideas* and ideology; *behavior* is rather different.

[21] I am preparing an analysis of this case. The relation of "courtly love" to social structure is complicated.

Why Love Must Be Controlled

Since strong love attachments apparently can occur in any society and since (as we shall show) love is frequently a basis for and prelude to marriage, it must be controlled or channeled in some way. More specifically, the stratification and lineage patterns would be weakened greatly if love's potentially disruptive effects were not kept in check. The importance of this situation may be seen most clearly by considering one of the major functions of the family, status placement, which in every society links the structures of stratification, kinship lines, and mate choice. (To show how the very similar comments which have been made about sex are not quite correct would take us too far afield; in any event, to the extent that they are correct, the succeeding analysis applies equally to the control of sex.)

Both the child's placement in the social structure and choice of mates are socially important because both placement and choice link two kinship lines together. Courtship or mate choice, therefore, cannot be ignored by either family or society. To permit random mating would mean radical change in the existing social structure. If the family as a unit of society is important, then mate choice is too.

Kinfolk or immediate family can disregard the question of who marries whom, only if a marriage is not seen as a link between kin lines, only if no property, power, lineage honor, totemic relationships, and the like are believed to flow from the kin lines through the spouses to their offspring. Universally, however, these are believed to follow kin lines. Mate choice thus has consequences for the social structure. But love may affect mate choice. Both mate choice and love, therefore, are too important to be left to children.

The Control of Love

Since considerable energy and resources may be required to push youngsters who are in love into proper role behavior, love must be controlled *before* it appears. Love relationships must either be kept to a small number or they must be so directed that they do not run counter to the approved kinship linkages. There are only a few institutional patterns by which this control is achieved.

1. Certainly the simplest, and perhaps the most widely used, structural pattern for coping with this problem is child marriage. If the child is betrothed, married, or both before he has had any opportunity

to interact intimately as an adolescent with other children, then he has no resources with which to oppose the marriage. He cannot earn a living, he is physically weak, and is socially dominated by his elders. Moreover, strong love attachments occur only rarely before puberty. An example of this pattern was to be found in India, where the young bride went to live with her husband in a marriage which was not physically consummated until much later, within his father's household.[22]

2. Often, child marriage is linked with a second structural pattern, in which the kinship rules define rather closely a class of eligible future spouses. The marriage is determined by birth within narrow limits. Here, the major decision, which is made by elders, is *when* the marriage is to occur. Thus, among the Murngin, *galle*, the father's sister's child, is scheduled to marry *due*, the mother's brother's child.[23] In the case of the "four-class" double-descent system, each individual is a member of *both* a matri-moiety and a patri-moiety and must marry someone who belongs to neither; the four-classes are (1) ego's own class, (2) those whose matri-moiety is the same as ego's but whose patri-moiety is different, (3) those who are in ego's patri-moiety but not in his matri-moiety, and (4) those who are in neither of ego's moieties, that is, who are in the cell diagonally from his own.[24] Problems arise at times under these systems if the appropriate kinship cell—for example, parallel cousin or cross-cousin—is empty.[25] But nowhere, apparently, is the definition so rigid as to exclude some choice and, therefore, some dickering, wrangling, and haggling between the elders of the two families.

3. A society can prevent widespread development of adolescent love relationships by socially isolating young people from potential mates, whether eligible or ineligible as spouses. Under such a pattern, elders

[22] Frieda M. Das, *Purdah* (New York: Vanguard, 1932); Kingsley Davis, *The Population of India and Pakistan* (Princeton: Princeton University Press, 1951), p. 112. There was a widespread custom of taking one's bride from a village other than one's own.

[23] W. Lloyd Warner, *Black Civilization* (New York: Harper, 1937), pp. 82–84. They may also become "sweethearts" at puberty; see pp. 86–89.

[24] See Murdock, *Social Structure*, pp. 53 ff. *et passim* for discussions of double-descent.

[25] One adjustment in Australia was for the individuals to leave the tribe for a while, usually eloping, and then to return "reborn" under a different and now appropriate kinship designation. In any event, these marital prescriptions did not prevent love entirely. As Malinowski shows in his early summary of the Australian family systems, although every one of the tribes used the technique of infant betrothal (and close prescription of mate), no tribe was free of elopements, between either the unmarried or the married, and the "motive of sexual love" was always to be found in marriages by elopement. B. Malinowski, *The Family Among the Australian Aborigines* (London: University of London Press, 1913), p. 83.

can arrange the marriages of either children or adolescents with little likelihood that their plans will be disrupted by love attachments. Obviously, this arrangement cannot operate effectively in most primitive societies, where youngsters see one another rather frequently.[26]

Not only is this pattern more common in civilizations than in primitive societies, but is found more frequently in the upper social strata. *Social* segregation is difficult unless it is supported by physical segregation—the harem of Islam, the zenana of India[27]—or by a large household system with individuals whose duty it is to supervise nubile girls. Social segregation is thus expensive. Perhaps the best known example of simple social segregation was found in China, where youthful marriages took place between young people who had not previously met because they lived in different villages; they could not marry fellow-villagers since ideally almost all inhabitants belonged to the same *tsu*.[28]

It should be emphasized that the primary function of physical or social isolation in these cases is to minimize informal or intimate social interaction. Limited social contacts of a highly ritualized or formal type in the presence of elders, as in Japan, have a similar, if less extreme, result.[29]

4. A fourth type of pattern seems to exist, although it is not clear cut; and specific cases shade off toward types three and five. Here, there is close supervision by duennas or close relatives, but not actual social segregation. A high value is placed on female chastity (which perhaps

[26] This pattern was apparently achieved in Manus, where on first menstruation the girl was removed from her playmates and kept at "home"—on stilts over a lagoon—under the close supervision of elders. The Manus were prudish, and love occurred rarely or never. Margaret Mead, *Growing Up in New Guinea,* in *From the South Seas* (New York: Morrow, 1939), pp. 163–66, 208.

[27] See Das, *Purdah.*

[28] For the activities of the *tsu,* see Hsien Chin Hu, *The Common Descent Group in China and Its Functions,* (New York: Viking Fund Studies in Anthropology, 10 (1948). For the marriage process, see Marion J. Levy, *The Family Revolution in Modern China* (Cambridge: Harvard University Press, 1949), pp. 87–107. See also Olga Lang, *Chinese Family and Society* (New Haven: Yale University Press, 1946), for comparisons between the old and new systems. In one-half of 62 villages in Ting Hsien Experimental District in Hopei, the largest clan included 50 per cent of the families; in 25 per cent of the villages, the two largest clans held over 90 per cent of the families; I am indebted to Robert M. Marsh, who has been carrying out a study of Ching mobility partly under my direction for this reference: F. C. H. Lee, *Ting Hsien. She-hui K'ai-K'uang t'iao-ch'a* (Peiping: Chung-hua p'ing-min Chiao-yu ts'u-chin hui, 1932), p. 54. See also Sidney Gamble, *Ting Hsien: A North China Rural Community* (New York: International Secretariat of the Institute of Pacific Relations, 1954).

[29] For Japan, see Shidzué Ishimoto, *Facing Two Ways* (New York: Farrar and Rinehart, 1935), Chapters 6, 8; John F. Embree, *Suye Mura* (Chicago: University of Chicago Press, 1950), Chapters 3, 6.

is the case in every major civilization until its "decadence") viewed either as the product of self-restraint, as among the 17th Century Puritans, or as a marketable commodity. Thus love as play is not developed; marriage is supposed to be considered by the young as a duty and a possible family alliance. This pattern falls between types three and five because love is permitted before marriage, but only between eligibles. Ideally, it occurs only between a betrothed couple, and, except as marital love, there is no encouragement for it to appear at all. Family elders largely make the specific choice of mate, whether or not intermediaries carry out the arrangements. In the preliminary stages youngsters engage in courtship under supervision, with the understanding that this will permit the development of affection prior to marriage.

I do not believe that the empirical data show where this pattern is prevalent, outside of Western Civilization. The West is a special case, because of its peculiar relationship to Christianity, in which from its earliest days in Rome there has been a complex tension between asceticism and love. This type of limited love marked French, English, and Italian upper class family life from the 11th to the 14th Centuries, as well as 17th Century Puritanism in England and New England.[30]

5. The fifth type of pattern permits or actually encourages love relationships, and love is a commonly expected element in mate choice. Choice in this system is *formally* free. In their 'teens youngsters begin their love play, with or without consummating sexual intercourse, within a group of peers. They may at times choose love partners whom they and others do not consider suitable spouses. Gradually, however, their range of choice is narrowed and eventually their affections center on one individual. This person is likely to be more eligible as a mate according to general social norms, and as judged by peers and parents, than the average individual with whom the youngster formerly indulged in love play.

For reasons that are not yet clear, this pattern is nearly always associated with a strong development of an adolescent peer group

---

[30] I do not mean, of course, to restrict this pattern to these times and places, but I am more certain of these. For the Puritans, see Edmund S. Morgan, *The Puritan Family* (Boston: Public Library, 1944). For the somewhat different practices in New York, see Charles E. Ironside, *The Family in Colonial New York* (New York: Columbia University Press, 1942). See also: A. Abram, *English Life and Manners in the Later Middle Ages* (New York: Dutton, 1913), Chapters 4, 10; Emily J. Putnam, *The Lady* (New York: Sturgis and Walton, 1910), Chapter 4; James Gairdner, ed., *The Paston Letters, 1422—1509*, 4 vols. (London: Arber, 1872-1875); Eileen Power, "The Position of Women," in C. G. Crump and E. F. Jacobs, ed., *The Legacy of the Middle Ages* (Oxford: Clarendon, 1926), pp. 414-16.

system, although the latter may occur without the love pattern. One source of social control, then, is the individual's own 'teen age companions, who persistently rate the present and probable future accomplishments of each individual.[31]

Another source of control lies with the parents of both boy and girl. In our society, parents threaten, cajole, wheedle, bribe, and persuade their children to "go with the right people," during both the early love play and later courtship phases.[32] Primarily, they seek to control love relationships by influencing the informal social contacts of their children: moving to appropriate neighborhoods and schools, giving parties and helping to make out invitation lists, by making their children aware that certain individuals have ineligibility traits (race, religion, manners, tastes, clothing, and so on). Since youngsters fall in love with those with whom they associate, control over informal relationships also controls substantially the focus of affection. The results of such control are well known and are documented in the more than one hundred studies of homogamy in this country: most marriages take place between couples in the same class, religious, racial, and educational levels.

As Robert Wikman has shown in a generally unfamiliar (in the United States) but superb investigation, this pattern was found among 18th Century Swedish farmer adolescents, was widely distributed in other Germanic areas, and extends in time from the 19th Century back to almost certainly the late Middle Ages.[33] In these cases, sexual intercourse was taken for granted, social contact was closely supervised by the peer group, and final consent to marriage was withheld or granted by the parents who owned the land.

Such cases are not confined to Western society. Polynesia exhibits a similar pattern, with some variation from society to society, the best known examples of which are perhaps Mead's Manu'ans and Firth's

---

[31] For those who believe that the young in the United States are totally deluded by love, or believe that love outranks every other consideration, see: Ernest W. Burgess and Paul W. Wallin, *Engagement and Marriage* (New York: Lippincott, 1953), pp. 217–38. Note Karl Robert V. Wikman, *Die Einleitung Der Ehe. Acta Academiae Aboensis (Humaniora)*, 11 (1937), 127 ff. Not only are reputations known because of close association among peers, but songs and poetry are sometimes composed about the girl or boy. Cf., for the Tikopia, Raymond Firth, *We, the Tikopia* (New York: American Book, 1936), pp. 468 ff.; for the Siuai, Douglas L. Oliver, *Solomon Island Society* (Cambridge: Harvard University Press, 1955), pp. 146 ff. The Manu'ans made love in groups of three or four couples; cf. Mead, *Coming of Age in Samoa*, p. 92.

[32] Marvin B. Sussman, "Parental Participation in Mate Selection and Its Effect upon Family Continuity," *Social Forces*, 32 (October, 1953), 76–81.

[33] Wikman, *Die Einleitung Der Ehe.*

Tikopia.[34] Probably the most familiar Melanesian cases are the Trobriands and Dobu,[35] where the systems resemble those of the Kiwai Papuans of the Trans-Fly and the Siuai Papuans of the Solomon Islands.[36] Linton found this pattern among the Tanala.[37] Although Radcliffe-Brown holds that the pattern is not common in Africa, it is clearly found among the Nuer, the Kgatla (Tswana-speaking), and the Bavenda (here, without sanctioned sexual intercourse).[38]

A more complete classification, making use of the distinctions suggested in this paper, would show, I believe, that a large minority of known societies exhibit this pattern. I would suggest, moreover, that such a study would reveal that the degree to which love is a usual, expected prelude to marriage is correlated with (1) the degree of free choice of mate permitted in the society and (2) the degree to which husband-wife solidarity is the strategic solidarity of the kinship structure.[39]

Love Control and Class

These sociostructural explanations of how love is controlled lead to a subsidiary but important hypothesis: From one society to another, and from one *class* to another within the same society, the sociostructural

[34] Mead, *Coming of Age in Samoa*, pp. 97–108; and Firth, *We, the Tikopia*, pp. 520 ff.

[35] Thus Malinowski notes in his "Introduction" to Reo F. Fortune's *The Sorcerers of Dobu* (London: Routledge, 1932), p. xxiii, that the Dobu have similar patterns, the same type of courtship by trial and error, with a gradually tightening union.

[36] Gunnar Landtman, *Kiwai Papuans of the Trans-Fly* (London: Macmillan, 1927), pp. 243 ff.; Oliver, *Solomon Island Society*, pp. 153 ff.

[37] The pattern apparently existed among the Marquesans as well, but since Linton never published a complete description of this Polynesian society, I omit it here. His fullest analysis, cluttered with secondary interpretations, is in Abram Kardiner, *Psychological Frontiers of Society* (New York: Columbia University Press, 1945). For the Tanala, see Ralph Linton, *The Tanala* (Chicago: Field Museum, 1933), pp. 300–303.

[38] Thus, Radcliffe-Brown: "The African does not think of marriage as a union based on romantic love, although beauty as well as character and health are sought in the choice of a wife," in his "Introduction" to A. R. Radcliffe-Brown and W. C. Daryll Ford, ed., *African Systems of Kinship and Marriage* (London: Oxford University Press, 1950), p. 46. For the Nuer, see E. E. Evans-Pritchard, *Kinship and Marriage Among the Nuer* (Oxford: Clarendon, 1951), pp. 49–58. For the Kgatla, see I. Schapera, *Married Life in an African Tribe* (New York: Sheridan, 1941), pp. 55 ff. For the Bavenda, although the report seems incomplete, see Hugh A. Stayt, *The Bavenda* (London: Oxford University Press, 1931), pp. 111 ff., 145 ff., 154.

[39] The second correlation is developed from Marion J. Levy, *The Family Revolution in China* (Cambridge, Harvard University Press, 1949), p. 179. Levy's formulation ties "romantic love" to that solidarity, and is of little use because there is only one case, the Western culture complex. As he states it, it is almost so by definition.

importance of maintaining kinship lines according to rule will be rated differently by the families within them. Consequently, the degree to which control over mate choice, and therefore over the prevalence of a love pattern among adolescents, will also vary. Since, within any stratified society, this concern with the maintenance of intact and acceptable kin lines will be greater in the upper strata, it follows that noble or upper strata will maintain stricter control over love and courtship behavior than lower strata. The two correlations suggested in the preceding paragraph also apply: husband-wife solidarity is less strategic relative to clan solidarity in the upper than in the lower strata, and there is less free choice of mate.

Thus it is that, although in Polynesia generally most youngsters indulged in considerable love play, princesses were supervised strictly.[40] Similarly, in China lower class youngsters often met their spouses before marriage.[41] In our own society, the "upper upper" class maintains much greater control than the lower strata over the informal social contacts of their nubile young. Even among the Dobu, where there are few controls and little stratification, differences in control exist at the extremes: a child betrothal may be arranged between outstanding gardening families, who try to prevent their youngsters from being entangled with wastrel families.[42] In answer to my query about this pattern among the Nuer, Evans-Pritchard writes:

You are probably right that a wealthy man has more control over his son's affairs than a poor man. A man with several wives has a more authoritarian position in his home. Also, a man with many cattle is in a position to permit or refuse a son to marry, whereas a lad whose father is poor may have to depend on the support of kinsmen. In general, I would say that a Nuer father is not

---

[40] E. g. Mead, *Coming of Age in Samoa*, pp. 79, 92, 97–109. Cf. also Firth, *We, the Tikopia*, pp. 520 ff.

[41] Although one must be cautious about China, this inference seems to be allowable from such comments as the following: "But the old men of China did not succeed in eliminating love from the life of the young women. . . . Poor and middle-class families could not afford to keep men and women in separate quarters, and Chinese also met their cousins. . . . Girls . . . sometimes even served customers in their parents' shops." Olga Lang, *Chinese Family and Society*, p. 33. According to Fried, farm girls would work in the fields, and farm girls of ten years and older were sent to the market to sell produce. They were also sent to towns and cities as servants. The peasant or pauper woman was not confined to the home and its immediate environs. Morton H. Fried, *Fabric of Chinese Society* (New York: Praeger, 1953), pp. 59–60. Also, Levy, *Family Revolution in China*: "Among peasant girls and among servant girls in gentry households some premarital experience was not uncommon, though certainly frowned upon. The methods of preventing such contact were isolation and chaperonage, both of which, in the 'traditional' picture, were more likely to break down in the two cases named than elsewhere."

[42] Fortune, *Sorcerers of Dobu*, p. 30.

interested in the personal side of things. His son is free to marry any girl he likes and the father does not consider the selection to be his affair until the point is reached when cattle have to be discussed.[43]

The upper strata have much more at stake in the maintenance of the social structure and thus are more strongly motivated to control the courtship and marriage decisions of their young. Correspondingly, their young have much more to lose than lower strata youth, so that upper strata elders *can* wield more power.

Conclusion

In this analysis I have attempted to show the integration of love with various types of social structures. As against considerable contemporary opinion among both sociologists and anthropologists, I suggest that love is a universal psychological potential, which is controlled by a range of five structural patterns, all of which are attempts to see to it that youngsters do not make entirely free choices of their future spouses. Only if kin lines are unimportant, and this condition is found in no society as a whole, will entirely free choice be permitted. Some structural arrangements seek to prevent entirely the outbreak of love, while others harness it. Since the kin lines of the upper strata are of greater social importance to them than those of lower strata are to the lower strata members, the former exercise a more effective control over this choice. Even where there is almost a formally free choice of mate—and I have suggested that this pattern is widespread, to be found among a substantial segment of the earth's societies—this choice is guided by peer group and parents toward a mate who will be acceptable to the kin and friend groupings. The theoretical importance of love is thus to be seen in the sociostructural patterns which are developed to keep it from disrupting existing social arrangements.

[43] Personal letter, dated January 9, 1958. However, the Nuer father can still refuse if he believes the demands of the girl's people are unreasonable. In turn, the girl can cajole her parents to demand less.

HUGO G. BEIGEL

Romantic Love

Romantic love is and will always remain a beautiful conception of the relation that ought to prevail between the sexes. Courtly love, derived from the court of Eleanor of Aquitaine, was codified and written down at that time in the treatise known as The Art of Courtly Love. *The book was written sometime between 1184 and 1186, and by the first quarter of the next century it had become widely known throughout Europe, its message being further extended through Western Europe by the troubadors, to whom we are indebted for the origins of our lyric poetry.[1]*

Dr. Beigel exonerates romantic love of the charge that it is responsible for the failure of many marriages; if anything, he suggests, it has greatly contributed to the success of many. He points out that what is confused with romantic love is sex. Although sex should not be demoted from its important place in human relations, it should not be identified or confused with love. *Sex should be a function of love, and not vice versa.*

As Dr. Beigel points out, it was Samuel Richardson, master printer and author of the first English novels, Pamela *(1740) and* Clarissa *(1747—1748), who first argued for natural feeling in the place of romantic reverie in marriage. The notion is, therefore, quite recent.*

The contribution of adolescent emotion and experience to the making of romantic love, most notably set out in the tragedy of Romeo and Juliet and developed in such works as Goethe's The Sorrows of Werther *(1774) and Rousseau's* La Nouvelle Héloïse *(1761), receives its due in this selection from Dr. Beigel—which is not always the case in discussions of the evolution of romantic love. By the end of the nineteenth century, as Dr. Beigel states, love had established itself as the principal prerequisite for marriage.*

Dr. Beigel has much to say about the role that love plays in the stressful,

"Romantic Love" by Hugo G. Beigel. From *American Sociological Review*, vol. 16, 1951, pp. 326–34. Reprinted by permission of the author and the American Sociological Association.

[1] For a more extended account of romantic love, see John Jay Parry's introduction to his translation of Andreas Capellanus, *The Art of Courtly Love* (New York: Columbia University Press, 1941).

competitive, and dehumanized world of today. It has, indeed, for most people become a last, rather than a first, resort.

The rise of the divorce rate, viewed as a threat to the marital institution, has led sociologists and psychologists to examine more closely current practices in marital selection. Owing to the emotional atmosphere surrounding this subject, however, the eagerness to provide an antidote has sometimes engendered premature conclusions. In particular has it become fashionable to point to "romantic love" as the villain in the picture. De Rougemont,[1] for instance, calls romance "a fever" and "a passing fancy" that is "the principal reason . . . for the growing number of divorces." A similar point of view is presented in several media intended for education in family and marital relations.[2]

Contrary to such verdicts, the hypothesis is here advanced that

1. courtly love and its derivative, romantic love, are not identical with puppy love,[3] but are expressions of a socio-psychological process that aims at the reconciliation of basic human needs with frustrating social conditions;

2. in this function romantic love has not only not harmed the relationship of the sexes but has enhanced the status of women and softened the impact on the marital union of factors that endanger the ideological basis of this and related institutions without providing substitute values.

Three phases of formalized love are discernible in Western culture. The first encompasses the origin of courtly love in the twelfth century, the second its revival at the turn of the nineteenth century, and the third its present state and significance for marital selection.

The first phase is called courtly love, *l'amoor de lonh* (distant love), or *minne*, and many literary documents, poems, and epics depict its form and the feelings involved. The history and practices of courtly love have been described by Folsom,[4] Gleichen-Russwurm,[5] Vedel [6] and others. We can thus confine ourselves to summarize merely the points essential to the present discussion.

[1] D. de Rougemont, "The Crisis of the Modern Couple," in R. N. Anshen, *Family, Function, and Destiny* (New York: Harpers, 1949), Chap. 16.

[2] H. Bowman, "This Charming Couple," 16mm. motion picture (New York: McGraw-Hill, 1950).

[3] E. W. Burgess and H. J. Locke, *The Family* (New York: American Book Co., 1950).

[4] J. K. Folsom, *Family and Democratic Society* (New York: Wiley, 1943).

[5] A. von Gleichen-Russwurm, *Kultur und Sittengeschichte aller Zeiten und Voelker* (Zurich: Gutenberg Verlag, 1920).

[6] V. Vedel, *Mittelalterliche Kulturideale, Natur und Geisteswelt* (Leipzig: 1916).

Courtly love was the conventionalization of a new ideal that arose in the feudal class and institutionalized certain aspects of the male-female relationship *outside marriage*. In conformity with the Christian concept of and contempt for sex, the presupposition for *minne* was chastity. Being the spiritualization and the sublimation of carnal desire, such love was deemed to be impossible between husband and wife. By application of the religious concept of abstract love to the "mistress," the married woman of the ruling class, who had lost her economic function, was endowed with higher and more general values: gentleness and refinement. Unselfish service to the noble lady became a duty of the knight, explicitly sworn to in the oath the young nobleman had to take at the dubbing ceremony.[7] Part of this service was ritualized; by means of such formalization the aggressiveness of unfulfilled cravings was channeled into codes and causes. In this manner sexual covetousness was deflected and the marital rights of husbands were—theoretically at least—safeguarded. This was obviously an important provision in an age in which social rules prevented free choice of a mate for marriage with the result that basic human needs were left unsatisfied.

Courtly love—in retrospect called romantic love—consequently was not a whimsical play. In spite of the surface appearance of its aesthetic formulation, it sprang from vital needs, from a deeply felt desire for the ennoblement of human relations, and from culture-bred frustrations. It made *māze* (moderation) a masculine virtue.

The fact that it is in the first place the sexual drive that was frustrated in this love relationship suggests an analogy with adolescent love. We can assume that certain features in the development of an adolescent brought up in an earlier phase of our culture coincide with tendencies observable nowadays. Those produced by the physiological maturation of the organism, for instance, are universal, and medieval literature gives some evidence of the emotions involved in self-discovery and the experience of change at this age.[8]

While the sexual drive rises to its greatest intensity during adolescence, it is denied satisfaction. Abstinence and celibacy being among the highest religious ideals and sexual immorality being threatened with hellfire, conflicts are created that lead to feelings of guilt, depreciation of the ego, and a heightening of the ego ideal. The phantasy is quickened and the suppression of the intensified desires

---

[7] "Monumenta Germaniae" (leges II, 363) in E. Sturtevant, *Vom guten Ton im Wandel der Jahrhunderte* (Berlin: Bong, 1917).

[8] Chretiens de Troyes, *Percival* (Conte del graal); Wolfram von Eschenbach, *Parzival*; Hartmann von Aue, *Der arme Heinrich*; Wirnt von Gravenberg, *Vigalois*.

results in a high emotionality which seeks for vicarious outlets.[9] While sexual relations cannot be established before marriage, there is sufficient erotic stimulation from talk, from visual stimuli, and an occasional trespassing with females outside one's class to feed the hope for more. Unless hope is realized or relinquished, the adolescent strains his resources to impress any members of the opposite sex and one female in particular whose behavior allows anticipation of possible acceptance. The means are display of masculine skill and prowess which, under the influence of religious teachings, the group code, and the masculine ideal, are subordinated to socially acknowledged causes or such feats as can be interpreted as good causes. The striving to prove one's independence and manliness finds expression in the search for adventures. The female, being at the same time the weaker competitor, the object to be obtained, and the substitute for the mother, grows to be the ideal audience and the representative for the super-ego; this has the effect that softer virtues often take precedence over coarser forms of behavior. While, in general, the adolescent does not aim at permanent possession of the female, any sign of approval by her is interpreted as acceptance and props up the wavering self-esteem. For this service she is idealized; even the refusal of sexual gratification is taken as an indication of greater self-control and moral strength. Such greatness, on the other hand, reflects favorably on the quality of the one accepted, who tries to live up to moral perfection and thus to the beloved's assumed higher standard. Vows of self-improvement alternate with feelings of unworthiness and moments of expansive self-feeling.

The adolescent's showing-off attitude has its counterpart in the medieval knight's search for adventures and in the tournaments he fought for his mistress. Love tests are frequent. Certain feats like those of Ulrich von Lichtenstein, who sent his little finger to his mistress and drank the water in which she had washed, or of Peire Vidal, who had himself sewn into a bear's hide and hunted,[10] have their parallels in the adolescent's obsessional yearning to impress the chosen female by valiance, self-sacrifice, and self-punishment. As do adolescent relations, courtly love provided partial satisfactions of the sexual desire. The lover having become a *drutz*[11] had the right to accompany his lady to

---

[9] K. C. Garrison, *The Psychology of Adolescence* (New York: Prentice-Hall, 1950); A. H. Arlitt, *Adolescent Psychology* (New York: American Book Co., 1933).

[10] H. Jantzen, ed., *Dichtungen aus mittelhochdeutscher Fruehzeit; Goeschen*, 137, Leipzig, 1910.

[11] Gleichen-Russwurm, *Kultur und Sittengeschichte*. The lover who has reached the fourth and highest state in the ritual of courtly love and is accepted.

her bedchamber, to undress her to the skin, and to put her to bed. Sometimes he was even allowed to sleep with her if he promised to content himself with a kiss. The love symbols are similar; the adolescent feels the one-ness with the beloved by wearing a lock of her hair or a ribbon near his heart as the knight felt it when he tied her veil around his armor; and as the mistress wore her gallant's blood-stained shirt so may a girl today wear her boy's pin, blazer, or baseball hat.

Such and many more similarities provoke the conclusion that courtly love represents the aesthetization of adolescent feelings which, though recognized as precious, are rarely experienced in adulthood with the same ardor. Under the influence of the cherished tales of oriental love refinement, the pyre of adolescent emotions was artificially kept burning, producing that subtler form of male-female relations that exploited the elations and depressions of enforced chastity for the ennoblement of the mind and gave the newly consolidated ruling class moral distinction over the crude indulgence of the masses.

The cultural significance of this concept lies in the fact that the idealization of the female initiated her social elevation and that it introduced voluntary fidelity, restraint, and the magnanimous gentleness of the male consciously into the relation between the sexes, qualities that were not considered essential or even possible in a marriage based on the semi-patriarchal concept of the Middle Ages. As the idea spread, it influenced greatly the emotional development of the group as a whole. This penetration became evident when romantic love, the bourgeois adaptation of courtly love, was propagated by the Romanticists.

Presupposing the knowledge of the historic and socio-economic roots of the Romantic movement,[12, 13] we limit ourselves again to an outline of those trends that have direct bearing on our subject.

In formulating the idea of romantic love, the Romanticists merely propounded a concept that had become a socio-psychological necessity. Starting in the fourteenth century, the dissolution of the broader family had progressed to the point where its economic, religious, and political functions were gone. With increasing urbanization the impact of social isolation made itself felt upon the individual. As a result of industrialization and mercantilization the father's authority had decreased and the children remained longer under the more emotionally oriented

[12] R. M. Meyer, *Die Literatur des 19. und 20. Jahrhunderts* (Berlin: Bondi, 1921).
[13] L. Walzel, *Romantik; Natur und Geisteswelt* (Leipzig, 1915), vols. 232, 233.

care of the mother, a fact that, together with the child's loss of economic function, effected a gradual change in personality, especially in the male personality. Reformation, revolutions, and wars had shaken the foundations of beliefs and traditions. Being the first to feel the pinch of the technological development on the treasured ideology of individualism, the Romanticists rebelled against the progressing de-humanization, the all-devouring materialism and rationalism, and sought escape from these dangers in the wonders of the emotions. In the basic feelings of humanity they hoped to find security and a substitute for the eliminated cultural values.

Under the increasing discomfort in a changing civilization, the aristocratic class had found a way to alleviate the defects of a family-prescribed monogamous marriage by dividing duty and satisfaction; the woman reserved her loyalty for her husband and her love for her gallant. Continuing on the tracks laid by the concept of courtly love, the nobles of the seventeenth and eighteenth centuries in Austria, Spain, France, the Netherlands, etc. still adhered to the tenet that love and marriage were irreconcilable. Yet, love had dropped its cloak of sublimation. The medieval concept had drawn a line between the spiritual and the animalic-sexual, between love and marriage. The court society of the Baroque[14] and the Rococo periods, by rewarding the gallant's deeds and duels with carnal favors, actually integrated sex and love—though only outside marriage. The adaptation noticeable in the ascending bourgeois class followed the same line—integration of sex and love—with the important difference that their economic struggle, their tradition of thrift, their religious ideas, (which, reformed to further their purposes, gave them moral support in their ultimate contest with the group in power)[15] did not permit them to accept illicit relationships as a solution of the problem. Yet, they had not remained unaffected by the ideology of earthly love. The refined concept had filtered down from the castles to the cities. Marriage, to be sure, was still arranged on a family basis with an eye on business, and the status of the wife was by no means enviable. But the verbiage of courtly love had entered the relation of the sexes. However, it was addressed not to the married woman, but, for the first time, to the marriageable maiden. Of course, this was hardly possible before the betrothal since, as an anonymous writer, Ursula Margareta, wrote in her diary

[14] M. Carrière, "Barocque," in Gleichen-Russwurm, *Kultur und Sittengeschichte,* vol. 11.
[15] R. H. Tawney, *Religion and the Rise of Capitalism* (Harmondsworth, England: Penguin Books, 1938).

published posthumously in 1805,[16] "the association with the opposite sex was not yet invented then (about 1760) . . . and we were shielded from them as from chicken pox." But during the months between engagement and marriage the betrothed was expected to "court" the girl and to display his emotional fervor in conversation, gifts, and poetry.

Preceded by the English novelist Samuel Richardson (1689–1761), who is credited with having said first that love is needed for marriage, the men of letters of those days pointed out both the immorality of the aristocratic solution and the sterility of the bourgeois pattern. Visualizing love as an antidote to the insecurity produced by social and technological changes, they propagated its legitimization and thus its perpetuation in marriage. The model for the bond between the sexes was the complex of feelings so graciously depicted in medieval romances, and its realization was henceforth called romance or romantic love.

We thus encounter a third stage in the development of love relations. The first admitted certain formalized features of adolescent feelings into the adult relationship to bridge the dichotomy between sublimated sex desires and the prevailing sex-hostile ideology; the second justified with love adulterous sex relations to ease the burden of an unreformed monogamy; the third aimed at the integration of love and marriage. It was promulgated by the first spokesmen of the bourgeois culture, who pleaded for the right of the young people to make their own choice for marriage on the basis of their feelings. No longer was there to be a cleavage between the spirituality of love and the marital sex relation, but the latter was to be sanctified by the former. This combination raised—though only ideologically at first—the woman of the middle class to the status which heretofore only the aristocratic lady had achieved in relation to the man.

Like courtly love, the concept of the Romanticists leaned noticeably on adolescent experiences. Though less ritualized than *minne,* romantic love acknowledged the value of certain pre-adult emotions. It established a hierarchy of characteristics that marked predestined affection. Foremost among them was emotional instead of rational evaluation, an attitude that contrasts clearly with the adult behavior normally aspired to, but is typical of adolescence, in which the rational powers do not operate at their optimum. Economic and status considerations were

---

[16] "Alte und neue Zeit; Taschenbuch zum geselligen Vergnuegen, 1805," reprinted in Sturtevant, *Vom guten Ton im Wandel.*

belittled. The female was idealized because of her ("natural") kindness, her intuition, and her nearness to nature. The male conceived of himself as a restless, striving, and erring deviate, spoiled by civilization, who, inspired by the female's love, might find the way back to his better self. This tendency corresponds to the adolescent's moments of magnified feelings of inferiority in the face of the female's greater poise and virtue and the elation when he is accepted nevertheless. While in the romantic concept the adventures of the mind were valued over fighting and fencing, conflict, self-recognition, sensitivity and the preservation of one's "true" and original self were elevated to moral qualities. The analogy to the adolescent's defensive attitude toward practical adult goals is evident.

The romantic love relationship itself was pervaded by melancholy and *Weltschmerz* (world-woe), another trend that is generally encountered in adolescence when the young person, having severed his emotional ties with his protective elders and craving new attachments, finds himself abandoned and, in comparison with the still child-like ego ideal, inadequate. From the same experience, on the other hand, results the claim to uniqueness and originality. Owing to his maturing mental powers, his broadening experience and knowledge, the adolescent frequently senses suddenly some of the discrepancies between reality and the moral teachings of his group, especially those which are antagonistic to the fulfillment of his desires. In this whirl of contradictions, wishes, rebellious emotions, and thoughts he feels like a castaway or like a revolutionary, chosen for the fight against either the traditions or the temptations, like a hero or like a sinner, full of defiance or full of resolutions to prove himself better than anyone else. Simultaneously proud and afraid of his discoveries, he seeks reassurance, someone to confide to, a companion who confirms the value of his ideas and thus of his personality.

Unable to turn to his parents, who in a quickly changing world are no longer considered revered guides but old-fashioned antagonists, he can find assurance only with a friend who seems to be shaken by similar convulsions and consequently "understands." After a period of homosexual friendships, the social conventions, the ideal of masculinity, and the sex drive usually direct the choice toward heterosexual relations, the same relations whose secrecy, mood of conspiracy, exuberations and depressions were the raw material for romantic love which, minimizing the sexual aspect, introduced friendship between the sexes.

By the end of the nineteenth century love had won its battle along the whole line in the upper sections of the middle class. It has since been regarded as the most important prerequisite to marriage. The American concept that considers individual happiness the chief purpose of marriage is based entirely on this ideology.

This fact must, however, not be confused with the allegations that the combination of romance and marriage is a specific American feature[17] or that marriage in this country is influenced to a unique degree by romantic love.[18] Doubtful as such assertions are in the absence of quantitative studies, they tend to create the impression that the majority of marriages are based on romantic love and that there is a deplorable causative relation between this circumstance and the record the United States holds regarding divorce. Actually, while estimates as to the frequency of love as a motive for marriage vary, marital counselors are agreed that love is more often presented as a reason for an intended marriage than feelings and circumstances warrant.

There arises, however, a second question. Is this love identical with the formalized concept of romantic love?

Certainly, the all-pervading melancholy is relatively rare among young adults; the mood of lovers, though still vacillating between joy and depression, is, on the whole, less sentimentally sad and, owing to their greater independence and the diminishing outside interference, is based more often on anticipation of marital joys, cooperation, "having fun together," and pursuit of common interests. As contact between the sexes is freer, partial sexual outlets are frequently provided. And while such activities may still be followed by feelings of guilt, these seem to be greatly attenuated by a presumed necessity caused by a socially cultivated sexual competition. Sex competition, on the other hand, particularly potent among girls, tends to blur the line between the excitations of love and those of an aggressive ambition. As a result of the prevailing dating convention and its concomitant early initiation of the sexes on a social basis, the over-idealization of the female (the keynote in both courtly and romantic love) is curbed. The love conventions of the twelfth and the nineteenth centuries were grants made by the man to the female; love in our day and in this country, conversely, has become a demand of the female, who is in the privileged position to extend or withhold sexual favors. Her own desire probably being lessened by culturally necessitated repressions, she

---

[17] Burgess, *The Family.*
[18] F. E. Merril, *Courtship and Marriage* (New York: Sloane Associates, 1949).

frequently uses such favors to reward or stimulate emotional expressions without regard to her own sex drive. Thus it appears that the modern love concept is not identical with romantic love, but is a derivative, modified in concord with the conditions of our age and based more on ego demands than on ideal demands.

But whatever form it takes, love is rarely the only consideration upon which marriage is contracted. Rather, it is one selective factor operating within the controls imposed upon the mates by our culture. These controls involve age, race, religion, ethnic origin, and class,[19] and the thus defined field is furthermore narrowed by regional proximity.

Under these circumstances, to blame love for the failures of marital unions in general is therefore unjustified, especially since a great number of marriages are contracted for reasons other than mutual love. In any case, however, the divorce rate cannot be taken as the sole indication of failure. In blaming its rise on the inadequacy of love as a selective agent, the judges omit several considerations, such as whether marriages contracted for economic or similar reasons do not work out worse and whether every failing marriage ends in divorce. Overlooked also is the fact that divorce is now more generally available than before. What marital life in the leading group looked like before the admission of either love or divorce can be gathered from any studies of the Baroque and Rococo periods. To give but one example: in 1716, Lady Montagu[20] wrote that in Vienna every woman of social standing had two men, her husband and her lover. Everyone knew of it and it was a serious offense to invite a lady to a party without asking both of her men.

Matters were similar for men in the higher social classes of all civilized countries with the exception of Spain where, in the seventeenth century, a man was said to have three women, his wife for representative purposes, his *manceba* (lady friend) for sexual, and his mistress for aesthetic conversations.[21] Thus, it was obviously not the combination of love and marriage that destroyed marital relations in Western culture.

Rather, the integration of love with marriage is an attempt at adjustment in the light of social concepts that outgrew the inadequate monogamous institution. Undoubtedly, love is not the panacea as

[19] A. B. Hollingshead, "Cultural Factors in the Selection of Marriage Mates," *American Sociological Review*, 15 (October, 1950), 619–27.

[20] Carrière, "Barocque."

[21] Sturtevant, *Vom guten Ton im Wandel.*

which it is sometimes presented. But it is less often the affectionate feeling that hampers the evaluation of the future mate's personality than it is the disregard of personality factors when the determination to get married results in confusing thwarted ambition or feelings of inferiority with love.

As with every institutionalized emotion, a certain amount of pretense is, of course, to be expected. Since love is considered the noblest motive for marriage, many people will profess love even though they have married for different reasons, family pressure, for instance, or material security or betterment of status.

But pretense need not be so evident. Sexual cravings are easily mistaken for love. As a matter of fact, love has attained an exceptional state with regard to sex. It has become the condition that allows the woman to lift the severe sex taboo imposed on her; the implicit supposition is that she may enter a sex relationship only when she is motivated by affectionate feelings. While this requirement is officially waived only when she marries, it frequently serves as an extenuating circumstance when she enters an illicit relationship. She certainly is judged differently when she succumbs to the latter for pecuniary considerations. As a result, the male uses the language and gestures of love to obtain temporarily desired sexual favors, and the female frequently interprets his "line" as love to avoid losing his attention.

Equally dangerous is self-deception. Especially in early marriages it happens often that undiluted adolescent feelings—such as the relief felt when the need to assert one's power and personality or one's independence, or the desire to escape depressing home restrictions is satisfied—are experienced as love and allowed to determine the selection of the mate. This tendency is greatly augmented since the motion picture industry, innumerable magazines and hack-written novels have undertaken to carry a cheap counterfeit of romantic love to the masses. The heroines of these products do not know of any attraction to a man except overwhelming, unconquerable, neurotic, and absolutely unselfish love that strikes at first sight, breaks down all bars of class or education, unfailingly cures all moral defects and inevitably solves all possible problems when it is transposed into marriage. Identifying herself with these stereotypes the young female movie-goer recognizes similarities between these and her own problems, and longing for the promised elations she views any approaching male under the aspect of marriage—the happy ending of the industrio-cultural literary products without any consideration of personality or moral values. Not being able to find the expected miracles in her mild likings, she tries to approximate her models by inflating her meager feelings. By autosuggestion and imitation she can usually convince herself of the unfathomable depth of her affection to anyone who speaks of love.

There is no doubt that such pressure-cooker recipes for happiness do not presage well for marriage. But such immature ideas cannot be blamed on love itself, nor can they minimize the function love has actually attained in selection for marriage. For with the collective aspect of marriage, family coherence, and the economic function of wife and offspring gone, there are no other positive agents left for mate selection except economic factors, sex, and personality assets.

The first, though important, does not guarantee satisfaction in the marital union. As a matter of fact, the intolerableness of the economic dependence of the female on the male has added impetus to the acceptance of the love concept. In our time, social and economic near-equality has given women sufficient independence to allow most of them a choice. They need not—at least not to the same extent as in former times—accept their husband's will and whim as their lot. With the social control weakened in this respect, only affection or considera-tion of the children can bind a woman to her husband.

Sex as a selective agent is ineffectual in our culture since the premarital testing of sexual compatibility is interdicted. Instead, the attraction produced by psycho-sexual emotions is taken as an indica-tion of mutual suitability. It does not, of course, fulfill this expectation, but feelings of love, of which this attraction is a part, are the closest substitute for tests. Even so, for the female whose training still compels her to repress all sex-tinged desires, it is, next to the psychotherapist, only love that helps her to overcome her inhibitions.

Similarly is it true that emotions provide no objective measurement for the future mate's personality. What love does, however, is to satisfy man's most urgent psychological needs, those produced by social isolation, by lack of any conceptual hold on the world in which he lives, and by lack of work satisfaction. Exposed to the high tensions of the modern work day and an unceasing brutal competition, man seeks relief in emotional satisfactions. Of these, few are available outside love. Reduced through technological progress to a negligible nut in an incomprehensible machine, confused by tumbling and contradictory moral values, he can regain the feeling of self-importance only in love. Only here can he find shelter from an inimical world, and, like the medieval knight take off his armor without fear. Only here can he be himself and expect to be accepted in all his imperfection and with all his unfulfilled secret yearnings.

Thus love—and only in connection with it marriage—has become the state from which compensation for all emotional frustrations is expected. True, such high expectations are likely to make the marital union precarious. It is doubtful, however, whether the imperfect remedy can be blamed for the illness. For, the emancipation of the female, her demand for mutuality of sex satisfactions, and the higher educational level of the middle classes have equally contributed to the brittleness of the marital institution. Yet, who would think of doing away with them even if he could?

Nor is it sensible to argue that marriage is irreconcilable with romance because sexual fulfillment and the intimacies of everyday life break down the idealization resulting from the sublimation of the sexual desire. Of course, the burning craving cannot last. But while it is true that the aura of divinity is not habit-resistant, it is also a fact that in a sexually gratifying relationship that has been built on love, that is, on understanding and mutual assistance in emotional conflicts, on moral support and common interests, on mutual confirmation and emotional security—unavailable anywhere else—the chance of creating an atmosphere of loyalty and friendship, tolerance and confidence are greater than in any other.

To summarize: courtly love, romantic love, and their modern derivative should be considered cultural phenomena evolved from basic human feelings that have gradually developed forms useful as replacements for discarded or decaying cultural concepts. Love aims at and assists in the adjustment to frustrating experiences. To measure its effect on marriage it must be judged in its true form and not in poor falsifications. Seen in proper perspective, it has not only done no harm as a prerequisite to marriage, but it has mitigated the impact that a too-fast-moving and unorganized conversion to new socio-economic constellations has had upon our whole culture and it has saved monogamous marriage from complete disorganization.

It is not impossible that with the progressing de-individualization inherent in our industrial orientation, sexual reproduction will some day be entirely divorced from individual personality preferences and based on a scientific biological-eugenic basis. So long, however, as human society has not taken this ultimate step, love provides one of the few positive factors in mate selection, allowing relief and emotional gratification in the enormous stress of civilization. It is not free of shortcomings; the solution, however, for the alleviation of ills concomitant to any cultural innovation and its integration with an old unreformed institution cannot be to dissuade young people from love, but only to aid them in the discrimination of those qualities in themselves and the prospective mate which must balance each other to ensure the satisfaction of emotional, sexual, and personality needs and, in so doing, the greater durability of their union.

ASHLEY MONTAGU

The Direction
of Human Development

In this contribution, which appeared as the final chapter in the author's book The
Direction of Human Development, *the essence of human nature in the light of
the scientific findings drawn from many different sources is summarized. Of all the
basic needs, the most important is considered to be the need for love—not merely to
be loved, but also to love others. The directiveness of human development is toward
love and cooperation, and when these needs are frustrated the organism, whether it
is a silkworm or a human being, becomes disordered and functions badly, if at all.*

*In the reading it is shown that the alleged incongruity between the world of
values and the world of fact is a myth brought about by a failure to understand the
nature of the human potentialities involved, that what is and what ought to be can
be perfectly reconciled once those facts are understood.*

*There is one thing, both in the book and in this selection from it, that I failed to
make clear, and that is that love is the highest form of intelligence, if we accept the
definition of intelligence as the ability to make the most appropriately successful
challenge to the particular situation. This is perhaps most beautifully exemplified by
the relationship of the loving mother to her child—when she is uninfluenced by the
advice of the "experts."*

> In the long run the fate of a civilization depends not on its political system,
> its economic structure, or its military might. Perhaps, indeed, all of these ulti-
> mately depend in turn upon the faith of the people, upon what we believe and feel
> about Man; about the possibilities of human nature; about our relation or lack of
> it to such intangibles as the meaning of morality or the true nature of Value.

—JOSEPH WOOD KRUTCH[*]

"The Direction of Human Development" by Ashley Montagu. Chapter 12 of Ashley
Montagu, *The Direction of Human Development*, rev. ed. (New York: Hawthorn Books, Inc.,
1970, pp. 288–317. Reprinted (with revisions) by permission of Hawthorn Books, Inc.

[*] Joseph Wood Krutch, "Speaking of Books," *New York Times Book Review*, August 16, 1953,
p. 2.

Human Nature

What is a human being? That is the question this book set out to answer, though the question was phrased differently. We set out by inquiring into the nature of man's original nature and the manner in which that nature is influenced and conditioned to assume a socially functional form.

The kind of answer each person or society returns to the question: "What is a human being?" will largely determine the health of such persons and societies. What human beings and their societies *do* about human beings is determined by the inner attitude motivating their outer acts.

In this last chapter let us recapitulate our main findings, and endeavor to draw the significant conclusions—conclusions which, in all humility, we hope may help humanity direct its own development toward the attainment of the optimum degree of health and happiness.

The Child Is Born Good

The age-old view that the human being is born "a natural barbarian," "an animal," "not naturally 'good' according to any standards set by civilized society"; that children are "*naturally* hostile," "little anarchists," "aggressive," "braggadocious and cruel," arises from the misinterpretations of the doctrine of "the Fall" or of "original sin." The reinforcement which these views received from nineteenth-century evolutionary biology and psychoanalytic theory in the first half of the twentieth century almost succeeded in hardening this view of the nature of human nature into something resembling an incontrovertible fact, a Law of Nature. Happily, in recent years, as a consequence of studies influenced both by developments in evolutionary biology and psychoanalytic theory, evidence has become available which indicates that the traditional view of human nature is unsound and, what is worse, capable of being profoundly damaging to human beings and to their societies. For this evidence indicates that human beings are born good—"good" in the sense that there is no evil or hostility in them, but that at birth they are wholly prepared, equipped, to function as creatures who not only want and need to be loved by others but who also want and need to love others. The evidence for these statements has been cited at some length in these pages. Let those who know of any evidence which controverts these statements bring it forth. I do not believe that such evidence exists.[1]

The belief is widely held by many students of human nature that human beings are born neither good nor evil but indifferent; that whether they become good or evil or both depends largely, if not entirely, upon the social conditioning they are made to undergo. This view sounds reasonable enough, but the evidence, I believe, when critically examined proves this view to be as unsound as the traditional view alleging the inherent brattishness or hostility of human nature.

The evidence cited in this book shows that the human organism at birth is a highly organized creature—*not* a disorganized, unready, unprepared, "wild" beast; that the newborn is highly organized to function as an increasingly growing-in-love harmonic bestower-of-benefits-upon-others, whose birthright, as an American philosopher has said, is development. The inner requirements of the infant are such as to cause him to want to be loved and to want to love others, and the basic needs of the infant are structured to function in this manner. The infant expects to have its needs satisfied, and when the infant's needs are satisfied it develops as a loving, cooperative, harmonic human being—that is, as a healthy human being. We have offered the definition of mental health as the ability to love, the ability to work, and the ability to play. The infant is equipped with the potentialities to develop all three capacities. How well a human being will develop his capacities to love, work, and play will depend largely upon the kind of training he will have received during infancy and childhood. The evidence shows, beyond any doubt, that the development of all the organism's potentialities for being human is a matter, reduced to its simplest elements, of certain kinds of stimulation and response: the stimulation of other human beings.

This stimulation, we have learned, must be of a certain kind. It must, in the first place, minister to and satisfy the needs of the infant. In order to minister satisfactorily to the needs of the infant it is desirable to know and understand the nature of those needs. In order to understand the nature of humanity and the direction of development which humanity may in future successfully pursue, it is indispensably necessary to understand the nature of the basic needs of the organism; these needs, whatever changes they may undergo,

---

[1] For a critical examination of the contrary view, see Ashley Montagu, ed., *Man and Aggression*, 2nd ed. (New York: Oxford University Press, 1973).

remain at the core essentially the same throughout life, from birth to death.

The nature of these needs has been discussed, and we have found that needs must be satisfied within reasonably short intervals and with certain frequencies—that it is not enough to "love" an infant three or four or five times a day, but that he must be loved for the greater part of the day—all the day—until he has had those inner securities built up within him which will later render it unnecessary for him to be in any way anxious about those stimulations which at the outset of his postnatal career are so indispensably necessary for his development.

As human beings we are the creators of human beings, and we shall always have the kind of human beings among us that we make. The role of chromosomes and genes should not be underestimated in the making of human beings, but the expression of the chromosomes and genes is to a certain extent under environmental control, and to the extent that we control the environment we control heredity, for heredity is the result of the interaction of the genes with environment. We cannot get more out of genes than we put into them or, to phrase this more constructively, we can get more out of genes than would otherwise be possible by providing them with environments in which they may optimally express themselves. Genes determine the limits of development under all environments; environments should therefore be provided which enable the human being to attain his fullest development within those limits.

Heredity, like constitution, is not as earlier generations thought it to be, the equivalent of predestination, but is the expression of that which is biologically given in interaction with that which is environmentally provided. Heredity should mean not Fate, but something about which we can, if we will, do a great deal. We shall not be able to substitute environment for genes, but we should always bear in mind that genes are not determiners of traits but of the responses of the developing organism to the environment. We can, therefore, always do something toward controlling the expression of those responses. It is good to know this, and it should serve to induce an optimistic mood. As E. L. Thorndike has remarked, "To the real work of man—the increase of achievement through improvement of the environment—the influence of heredity offers no barrier."

The making and molding of human beings as human beings is in our power as human beings. Because this is so, the direction of human development, of human evolution, is within our power as human beings—for good or evil. It is necessary, then, that we shall make quite certain that the direction of that development shall be good and neither evil nor confused.

What Is Good?

The evidence we have now considered tells us that "good" is whatever the person does that confers survival benefits upon others in a manner which contributes to their ability to love, to work, and to play—in other words, to their ability to do likewise to and for other human beings. Human welfare is whatever contributes to the maintenance and development of human health—the ability to love, the ability to work, and the ability to play.

To the extent that any person departs in his behavior from the undeviating practice of his capacity for love, work, and play, to that extent we would have reason to believe that forces inimical to his healthy functioning are at work in him. We should seek to understand those forces and remedy them by providing the person with those conditions of life which will most contribute toward his healthy functioning. It should be one of the purposes of education to make human beings understand the nature of human goodness, and what it is that must be done to develop such goodness as has already been developed in one by one's educators. It should be the primary purpose of all human societies to provide those conditions which shall make it possible for as many human beings as possible to function as human beings. This constitutes the answer to the question "Education for what?"

What the human organism requires most for its development is a nutriment of love; the source of virtually all health is in the experience of love, especially within the first six years of life. No matter how well the needs of the human organism are physically satisfied, unless the physical satisfaction of those needs is accompanied by love, the human organism will not develop satisfactorily; that is to say, it will not develop as an organism that has been so harmonically satisfied that its principal interest lies in satisfying others. After all, this is what most of us want most of all to do all our lives, however confusedly or not we may recognize it: to satisfy others. The tragedy is that so many of us have failed to learn, because we had not been properly taught, how to satisfy others. To be rejected at any age because those who have been responsible for us have failed to teach us how to love others is, perhaps, the most unkind of all the inhumanities which we commit against others.

The child who is unloved does not develop properly; he may even sicken and die principally as a consequence of insufficient love. Some children manage to survive under the most barren human conditions—we do not yet know why.[2] Some day we shall study such children and discover the answer, but it would appear that most, if not all, children suffer seriously crippling effects when exposed to an inadequate diet of love. There has here been cited but a fraction of the evidence supporting these statements. The material now available showing the fundamental importance of love for the healthy development of the human being is of considerable proportions.

From all this material it seems now clear that the main principle by which human beings must guide the future course of their development is love. It is, therefore, of the first importance that we be clear as to the meaning of love.

What Is Love?

Love is that form of behavior which contributes to the healthy development of both the lover and the loved. By healthy development is meant the increase in the capacity to function as a totally harmonic person who confers creatively enlarging benefits upon all with whom he comes into association. Love, it would seem, is the principal developer of the potentialities of being human; it is the chief stimulus to the development of social competence, and the only quality in the world capable of producing that sense of belongingness and relatedness to the world of humanity that every healthy human being desires and develops.

Love is creative, both for the receiver and the giver. Genuine love can never harm or inhibit—it can only benefit and create freedom and order. Love has a firmness and a discipline of its own for which there can be no substitute. No child can ever be spoiled by genuine love, and there are few if any human problems which cannot be efficiently solved by its application.

We may tentatively set out below the qualities and characteristics of love, upon which most students of the subject seem to be agreed.

[2] See Ashley Montagu, *The Elephant Man* (New York: Ballantine Books, 1973).

The Qualities and Characteristics of Love

- *Love implies the possession of a feeling of deep involvement in another, and to love another means to communicate that feeling of involvement to him.* Essentially this means that while love begins as a subjective state, it must be activated and made objective; that is, it must be demonstrative if it is to be fully realized. Love is not passive—it is active; it means involvement.

- *Love is unconditional—it makes no bargains and trades with no one for anything.* It is given freely and without any strings attached. It says, in effect, to the loved one: "I am for you because you are you—and not because you are going to be something I want or expect you to be, but simply because you are you as you now are."

- *Love is supportive.* It conveys to the loved one that he can depend upon those who love him, that they will always be standing by to give him the support he most needs, with no questions asked, neither condemning nor condoning, but endeavoring sympathetically to understand, that no trust will be misused; that no faith will be broken; that he will never under any circumstances be failed in his needs.

- *Love is firm.* Love is characterized by a firmness and integrity which not only conveys a feeling of security to the loved one, but serves also as a discipline in that it helps the loved one to respond in kind. But love continues even though we know that the loved one may never respond in kind. The firmness of love conveys to the loved one that both one's "Yea" and "Nay" are equally the firm evidence of one's love. The loved one, therefore, comes to incorporate this kind of firmness within himself.

> Let me not to the marriage of true minds
> Admit impediments. Love is not love
> Which alters when it alteration finds,
> Or bends with the remover to remove:
> O, no! it is an ever-fixéd mark,
> That looks on tempests and is never shaken;
> It is the star to every wandering bark,
> Whose worth's unknown, although his height be taken.
> Love's not Time's fool, though rosy lips and cheeks
> Within his bending sickle's compass come;
> Love alters not with his brief hours and weeks,
> But bears it out even to the edge of doom.
>   If this be error and upon me prov'd,
>   I never writ, nor no man ever lov'd.

So wrote William Shakespeare.

- *Love is most needed by the human organism from the moment of birth.* Our evidence indicates that love is the birthright of every human being, the birthright indispensably necessary for the optimum development of the person. It seems to be clear that the best environment, in which love is most efficiently and satisfactorily provided, is within the warm ambience of the bosom of the family. The pattern of love which the child learns within the family, if he learns it well, he will later extend to all human beings.

- *Love is reciprocal in its effects, and is as beneficial to the giver as it is to the recipient.* To love another means to love oneself as well as the other; in this sense love is the highest form of selfishness as well as the highest form of unselfishness, the best of all forms of conduct for the development of self, one's own self and the selves of others.

- *Love is creative* in that it actively participates in the creative development of the loved one as well as contributing toward the further development of the lover.

- *Love enlarges the capacities of those who are loved* and of those who love so that they become increasingly more sensitive in probably all areas of their being.

- *Love continually elicits, by encouragement, the nascent capacities of the loved one.* In the absence of love those capacities will either fail altogether to be elicited or fail of healthy development. For example, the capacity to feel sensitively, to feel warmly toward others, the capacity to perceive rapidly the changing character of a situation, the capacity to identify with others, the ability to adjust rapidly to rapidly changing conditions, and the like. In all these capacities the person who has been loved is more efficient than the person who has been inadequately loved.

- *Love is tender,* with a tenderness that abjures every form of insensitivity and every form of violence.

- *Love is joyful*—it is pleasure-giving, happiness-producing; it is goodness itself. This does not mean that love is necessarily associated with states of ecstasy or gaiety. Love may produce temporary states of nonpleasure or displeasure, as for example, in children and others who are forbidden some immediate satisfaction for their own "good." Prohibitions stemming from love contribute to the development of the capacity for love and mature character.

- *Love is fearless.* Love has no element of fear in it, and produces no fear in others. Love braves all conditions and situations in a security-producing manner; hence, love tends to reduce fear, allay suspicion, soften all harshness, and produce peacefulness.

- *Love enables the person to treat life as an art* which the person, as artist, is continually seeking to improve and beautify in all its aspects.

- *Love as an attitude of mind and as a form of behavior is adaptively the best and most efficient of all adjustive processes in enabling the human being to adapt himself to his environment.*

• *For the person and for the species love is the form of behavior having the highest survival value.*

Adequate love is necessary for the adequate physical growth and development of the human organism, as well as for its adequate mental growth and development. Intelligence as well as mental health is furthered by the contributions which love makes to the developing person. In love, in short, we have discovered the touchstone and the compass by which man may guide his own most successful course through the shoals and reefs of this life, instead of being tossed about, as he has in the past, and as he is at present, in a rudderless boat upon a mysterious and uncompassionate sea.

To live as if to live and love were one is not a new recommendation; what is new is that the meaning of love should have been rediscovered in the twentieth century by scientific means. Every people has its equivalent of the Sermon on the Mount, and our churches have constantly reminded us of the existence of love and enjoined us to practice it. This being so, it may well be asked why it is that we seem so monumentally to have failed to realize such injunctions? Why is it that there have been so many members of churches but so few lovers? Why is it that there are so many Christians but so few followers of Jesus?

The answer, it seems to me, is that we have been miseducated out of the capacity to be lovers of our fellow human beings, and that we have on the other hand been confusedly trained to keep our eye on the main chance. For the most part this has been the secular training of Western man. We have tended to live by false values, and to transmit these values to the young. We have tended to make egotists of creatures who are biologically organized to function most efficiently as altruists. The evidence indicates that from birth onward the direction of the human being's drives is toward cooperation, and that healthy development consists principally in the encouragement of the optimum fruition of these drives. If, as in the Western world we have largely been doing, we interfere with the development of those drives by opposing to them requirements that are antagonistic toward the development of cooperativeness, these drives tend to become deformed and weakened, while at the same time conflicts are engendered within the psyche which produce great personal and social disoperativeness.

It appears, then, that whatever contributes toward personal and social health and happiness is good and desirable for human beings, and that whatever contributes to the contrary is bad and undesirable for human beings. In short, whatever militates against or is opposed to the development of the tendencies toward cooperation in the person and in the society militates against and is opposed to the healthy development of the person and of the society. In essence this is to say that uncooperativeness or unlovingness is the worst of all the sins which one human being can commit against another.

In this volume we have, I hope, sufficiently explored the meaning and requirements of cooperation to be able to take for granted what it is that human beings must cooperate with. Perhaps it will bear repeating in a phrase: What human beings must cooperate with is the desire of other human beings to be loved—to be cooperated with. One cannot secure love by seeking it, but only by giving it. Having discussed and set out the criteria of love, of loving, there should be no difficulty in understanding what it is that requires to be done: Human beings must be satisfied in their need for love. The direction of human development lies in and through the course of love; all else is secondary to this. The primacy of love is unchallengeable—and unchallengeably clear as the first requirement of human development. All the agencies of socialization should be based upon the understanding of this fact. Because all agencies of socialization are educative, education constitutes the key to the solution of the ills of humanity, and the means by which all the potentialities of the organism for being human may be unlocked. Hence the importance of understanding the meaning of man for education and the meaning of education for man.

Education and Human Relations

In keeping with the general materialization of Western man and the high value placed upon techniques, education has progressively degenerated into instruction. It is not unlikely that if, in the Western world, we go on as we have been doing in the immediate past, in a generation or two scarcely anyone will remain who understands the difference between education and instruction. Instruction is the process of pumping information into the person—it literally means "to build into"; whereas education, *educare*, means the process of nourishing or rearing a child or young person, in the sense of the Latin word to which it is related, *educere*, to lead forth. We must recognize that today, in the Western world, we have far too much instruction and too little education. We are far too busy filling up the young with what we think they ought to know, to have much time left over for helping them become what they ought to be. There is after all, a difference between *knowing* and *being*—it is better to be more than one seems and to be wise rather than knowledgeable. We pump in the information in the hope that somehow the recipients will know what to do with it or what it is for, and that somehow this procedure will make the beneficiaries of it realize their potentialities. By this means we naively suppose that human beings will learn how to distinguish the good from the bad and to act accordingly, that by this means they will learn how to use their minds and evaluate evidence critically, that by this means they will become better persons and better citizens. Never have we been more mistaken—as the record shows.

In the United States for the year ending in 1974 we find certifiable mental illness to exist in 1 out of every 4 families; we find that a murder was committed every 72 minutes during the day; that during every hour of the day there were 15 crimes of violence—stabbings, shootings, clubbings; that during every hour of the day there were 7 robberies and 26 cars stolen. What is perhaps worse than all this, if it could be worse, is that 1 out of every 43 children has a police record. Juvenile delinquency, broken homes—1 out of every 3 marriages ends in divorce or separation—these are all tragic evidences of the failure of education—education primarily in the home and secondarily in the school. This is perhaps not surprising in a land in which of our total national income 5 percent was expended on alcoholic beverages as compared with approximately 3 percent spent on education.

Education—Teachers and Parents

We have made a fundamental error in distinguishing what goes on in the training of children in the home from what goes on in the training of the young in the schools. Education begins at birth, and the parents are the first educators, the mother usually being the principal of the parental educators. Because the first half-dozen years of the child's life are so critically important for its development there can be little doubt that the parents, and in particular the mother, constitute the most important educators in the life of the person. Hence, if any distinction is to be made between parental and school education it should be in terms of emphasis upon the supreme importance of the first six years of the child's life. This, however, in no way implies that the education of a human being is a discontinuous process, with a first part at home and a second part at school. On the other hand, education must be regarded as a continuous process, and it should be based upon a single and unitary viewpoint as to its nature and purposes in which everyone, parents and teachers, participate *together*.

Education is the process of teaching human beings to live in ways which contribute to the welfare of their fellow human beings. The theoretical background emerging out of the facts we have discussed in this book with respect to the meaning of "welfare" has already been examined at sufficient length. If the analysis of the facts is sound and the theory is likewise sound—as I believe it to be—then it is clear that the most important function of education is to cultivate and develop the potentialities of the child for being a loving human being. The evidence suggests that the status of a loving human being is the most desirable and important that a human being can achieve. To produce loving human beings should be the primary purpose of education, and all else should be secondary to that purpose. Reading, writing, and arithmetic are but skills, techniques, means, which should be designed to assist the loving human being to realize to the optimum his potentialities for getting the most out of life by putting the most into it. Reading, writing and arithmetic are not ends in themselves but secondary means—means to the end of realizing the fullest richest life possible within the limits of the abilities of each human being. Such skills are secondary to the main purpose of living—which is life, a life that is worth living insofar as it realizes its highest form in the developed loving human being.

In our schools we pay lip-service to such an ideal of education, but in practice we teach *subjects,* we no longer teach human beings. Too much of our attention is devoted to problems of discipline, so that for many teachers their task has reduced itself to one of baby-sitting, for the original baby-sitters—the parents—who have failed to sit as they ought to have done. This problem has become so serious in the United States that in many high schools a permanent squad of police has been installed in order that some semblance of discipline shall be maintained! Perhaps these are extreme cases; in any event they are mentioned here in order to underscore, as it were, the kind of disciplinary problems with which the school is faced, which under a reasonable system of education would never in the first place have arisen.

A patient, in searching for an explanation for his mental illness, remarked: "My mother's impulses never seemed to correspond to my needs." This probably represents a sound statement of the origin of many mental disorders, and it may be profitably paraphrased in the statement that the impulses of many educators seem rarely to correspond to the needs of the young. This is not difficult to understand when one realizes that what the young want is principally to be stimulated in their need for human development, whereas too many teachers are engaged in filling them up with a number of subjects which to the child appear to be quite unrelated to his most fundamental needs. What is human learning if not the development of the needs for being human?

Almost all children find their lives in school puzzlingly unrelated to their lives at home. This should not be so. School should constitute a continuation and an enlargement of the experience that begins in the home and terminates in the world outside, only to be renewed again in the home and once more reinforced—as it should be—in the school, and so on until one's education is completed . . . if one's education ever is completed. The love that should and often does exist between parents and children—though it is more often found between mother and child—is the model and the pattern of the human relationship that should exist between all human beings. So that there be no misunderstanding as to my meaning, let me say that I mean exactly what these words imply; namely, that human beings should love each other as a mother loves her children, and that this should be possible for males as well as for females, whether they have ever biologically engendered children or not. But whether the male will learn to love as a parent or in any other capacity will depend largely upon his mother, for as La Barre points out, "The human male has no instincts, and no anatomy to teach him to love a child as such. If the male learns the pleasures of paternity as opposed to those of procreation, it is the result of the mother's teaching him."

But how is it possible—to take but one instance—it may be asked, and indeed is it desirable, for members of the opposite sex to fall in love with one another, to love each other as a mother loves her child? The answer is that it is both possible and desirable. The love that should and can exist between male and female should consist in a developed form of maternal love in which all the elements of maternal love persist. A man should love a woman with the tenderness, respect, and care for her welfare with which a mother loves her child, but in addition he should be drawn to and love her for her qualities as a whole. Her external attractions, whatever their nature, may initiate the process but they should never constitute the *end* of it.

This is a different conception of love between the sexes from the romantic and prevailing erotic view. Contemporary love between the sexes is mainly sexual, the male being drawn toward the female principally through the stimulus-valve of her curvilinear properties, the female, under the influence of selection pressure, generally settling for a male largely on the basis of his market value as a scarcity commodity, provided also he is someone who, with all his faults, one can like or learn to like.

Too many persons in our Western cultures confuse a sexual attraction with love. As long as the opposite partner remains physically attractive, the psychophysical disturbances the subject feels are equated with love. But such disturbances are no more akin to love than cupidity is to Cupid. Under such environmental conditions, when the physical attractiveness ceases "love" also ceases. Such "love" is, of course, not love, but a crass sexuality. Such persons are sexual without being loving, whereas the loving person cannot be sexual without loving.

The essence of love between the sexes is the tender regard, respect, and care for the other person's welfare—and if it is not that, then whatever else it is, it is not love.

For a healthy human being it is possible to be as much interested in another's welfare as a mother is in her child's. There is a tender regard and involvement in such a person's interest in other human beings which has but to be experienced for it to be understood how well some persons have achieved this maternal capacity for love, even of the stranger. It is in the development of this maternally based capacity for love that the future of humanity lies. Until this truth is fully understood and practiced, so far as the direction of human development is concerned, almost all other activities will remain in comparison diversionary and stultifying. It must be the task of educators to awaken to this truth, and what it is that requires to be done to realize it.

The school, like the home, must become an experience in the growth and development of one's capacities for becoming a loving human being. But in addition, the school has to provide the child with the necessary equipment, the technique and skills, with which he can the more satisfactorily realize—creatively realize—his potentialities for contributing to the welfare of his fellow human beings. The greatest gift the teacher can offer the child is himself—the teacher's own being. A good teacher must mean something to himself if he is to mean anything to his pupils, and he can mean no more to his pupils than he means to himself. Hence, the value of a good teacher is exceeded by nothing, unless it be the value of a good parent. But when we truly understand the meaning of good teaching it is realized that the good parent is essentially a teacher, and that the good teacher is essentially a parent. How much of what is good in us do we not owe both to parents and to teachers? Where parents fail, teachers often succeed. In a period when many of those who act as parents are not the biological genitors of their children it has become apparent that the complex feelings of parentage have no necessary connection with biological parentage, that between persons who are biologically not kin the deepest feelings of kinship can develop.

There are some who have suggested that it would be a desirable thing to abolish social parentage. This is silly. What we need to do is not to abolish social parentage but to deepen and extend our conception of it. Teachers should stand to their children *in loco parentis.* As the child's parents are its domestic parents, so at school the teacher should be to the child its school parents. I am suggesting that we deepen and extend the kinship system, not in terms of classificatory relationships, but in terms of changes in attitudes. All adults, particularly teachers of the young in the schools, should take a parental interest in the welfare of children. Unfortunately, in the past the attitude of the teacher to the child often resembled that of the company sergeant to the newly inducted private. We have seen that when the sergeant behaves as a reassuring parental figure to the men in his charge their mental health and their efficiency under battle conditions are greatly improved. It is not only schoolteachers, but teachers of every kind who have this lesson to learn: To teach well, one must love one's pupil as a mother loves her child. There have been some teachers who have grasped the truth of this principle, and they have unexceptionally been the great teachers; perhaps the greatest of them all was and is Heinrich Pestalozzi (1746–1827). It was Pestalozzi who said that "Love is the sole and everlasting foundation on which our nature can be trained to humaneness." And it was Pestalozzi who wrote: "The good instincts of mankind, in their pure state, are more than gifts of art or chance. Their fundamental qualities lie deeply buried in man's nature. All men feel the need to develop these powers, and the paths along which Nature reveals them must be kept clear and easy of access. To achieve wisdom and tranquility, the processes of human education must be kept simple and of universal application."

It is through love that teachers of every kind, whether they be actual or derived parents, must seek to develop those fundamental qualities and powers of which Pestalozzi speaks along the paths which Nature reveals. We need to recall, in the words of Francis Bacon, that Nature in order to be commanded must be obeyed. If, then, what has been adumbrated in this book as the nature of human nature, the requirements for the development of human nature, is sound it will be understood that learning and being loved are more closely interrelated conditions than has hitherto been clearly understood. This, perhaps, indicates a more intensive statement of the law or reinforcement. To live, to learn, and to love—these are the three great chords of being; to unify them into a harmonic series requires the skill of an artist. Life regarded as a public performance on the violin, during which one must learn the instrument as one goes along, rarely results in anything more than an unhappy fiddler. A human being should be a work of art. He can be turned into a work of art by other human beings who are artists, and thus learn to become an artist himself, an artist who, in turn, works continually to improve himself and help others to improve themselves. Knowing what is to be done, how else can one better achieve what is to be realized than with the tenderness and loving care of a mother?

All of us are to some extent the product of the maternal principle. The next best thing to being a mother is to behave like one. And by behaving like a mother, we of course mean the possession of those attitudes of mind which condition one to behave toward others as a mother does toward her child. Perhaps the English, the Germans, and the Japanese are the peoples who have most departed from this ideal, for that there has been a departure is suggested by the fact that many nonliterate peoples such as the Eskimo and the Australian aborigines —to name two of the most primitive—have pretty closely approximated to the realization of this ideal. Not all earlier men may have been cooperative and loving, but that many of them were there can be no reasonable doubt. The Italians and the French are somewhat more influenced, in their human relations, by the maternal principle, but these peoples are far from having learned the lesson completely. Indeed, their recent history indicates a significant deterioration. And yet to the extent that the Italians and the French retain their warmth they are warmer than the English, the Germans, and the Japanese. It is no accident that these latter peoples make the most efficient soldiers. One of the kindest and most significant things one can say about any people is that they make poor fighters. It is not by fighting that any human problem will ever be solved, any more than any child will ever be improved by spanking, rather than by love and by the understanding which is love.

There burns a pure flame within us; that flame is love. It is the source from which we draw and convey our warmth to others. It is the light which guides us in relation to our fellow men; it is the flame before which we warm the hands of life, and without which we remain cold all our lives. It is the light of the world. The light which it casts enables us clearly and unambiguously, unfalteringly, to see our relation to our fellow men. It is the task of teachers to keep that flame alive, for if they fail to do that, there is a real danger that the light may go out of the world.

Our present educational and social failure to recognize the new bases of human relationships must change if we are to survive—nothing less than that. We must cease doing violence to human nature. By doing violence to human nature we have produced the unique paradox of the creature who, by nature capable of being the most loving and peaceful, has been turned into the most destructively violent on the face of the earth. Our shattered values have made the horrible, devastating threat of an atom bomb world a reality. Clearly, we need to know at least as much about the maker as about the manufacture of atom bombs.

Human beings who are torn and distracted by internal insecurities and anxieties, who are conditioned to love their neighbors on Sundays and to compete with them on weekdays, cannot long survive. A nation of such persons must eventually founder on the reefs of its own false values. External defenses can never make up for the lack of internal controls. What needs to be done is to develop internal controls in human beings so that they can withstand external pressures and maintain internal equilibrium. This can never be achieved by doing violence to their nature. It can only be done by strengthening those basic needs with which all human beings are born—not by frustrating them. It is these basic needs that provide us with the basic values which human beings must seek to satisfy and fulfill if they are to live and function in optimum health and happiness.

Values, Ethics, Education, and the Good Life

A value is the judgment of the quality of an experience. Such value judgments are biologically based in and originally constituted by the basic needs of the organism, and all other needs—secondary, tertiary, and so on—are eventually built up upon the functioning of these needs. Values are in essence guides to need-gratifications. The experiences that will gratify my needs create my values, therefore the structure and functioning of my needs determine the range and limits of my values. I must have oxygen to gratify my need for air, but whether that oxygen comes to me in a tent, a house, a factory, a mine, or in a stratoliner, and whether it varies all the way from pure to polluted will depend upon accidental conditions that must neither fall below nor exceed certain limits. Within these limits, which my biological needs determine, I can adapt myself to any atmospheric conditions. And so it is for all other needs. The experiences that will not gratify my needs are negatively valued by me—these, too, are values. My judgment of the quality of these experiences and my acceptance of them or not will largely be determined by my organismal needs—needs that I share with all other human beings.

The supreme value is love, and if we use this as our touchstone of value we cannot possibly go wrong. Man is the evaluating animal, and he evaluates on the basis of his needs. Every human being is born a creature that evaluates all experience in terms of the desire to be loved and the desire to love. We at long last have thus arrived at an understanding that there do exist certain universal values, and that these are born with every human being. "What is right is what is right for human nature." It was Aristotle who declared that the important thing about the nature of man is not what he is born *as*, but what he is born *for*. In order to know what a man is born *for* it is indispensably necessary to understand what he is born *as*, and when we understand what he is born *as* we will better be enabled to assist him to realize what he is born *for*.

Because we now have some understanding of the basic structure of human nature, we are at least in a position to be able to test our theory. The basic needs are not logical inferences but factual phenomena; they *ought* to be satisfied if the organism is to survive or develop, and that *oughtness* is as much a fact and lies as much in the world of *is* as do the basic needs themselves. "Ought" is in this case merely a way of denoting a necessary response—which, again, falls within the world of *is*. As Arnold Brecht has so well put it, "Thus it is a factual statement rather than a logical inference when we say that feeling some specific requiredness as an *ought* is part of our human equipment. This urge, this demand, this *ought*, whatever its value and validity, is a factum, a datum, found in the world of *is*. It would be so even if only a part of mankind felt this *ought* as such. Here is the bridge, or one bridge, between *is* and *ought*." The nature of the basic needs conditions the oughtness of the responses; what ought to be is what the basic needs determine, and what they determine we are now for the first time able to decipher. In the nature of the basic needs we have the Rosetta Stone which translates for us into the vernacular what the direction of human development ought to be, what, indeed, it must be if the human race is to survive.

But much more than survival is involved. What is involved is the realization of the potentialities for goodness of all human beings everywhere for the greatest good of all humanity—the unbridgeable gap between *ought* and *is*, when we look at what *is* in terms of what we know the basic needs to determine, and at what *ought* to be if human beings are to develop in optimum health and happiness. To realize the good life in the person and behavior of each human being, our evidence indicates that each human being must be adequately loved—that is to say, he must have his needs adequately satisfied for being loved and loving others. Such human beings will create institutions and societies which will be the best that human beings can possibly create and, within whatever limitations those societies operate, they will remain infinitely perfectible. Utopia would not at once descend upon the earth, nor would all human problems immediately be solved. But under such conditions they would become more capable of solution than they have yet ever been.

The reciprocal adaptation that human beings make to one another in terms of love is the basic adaptation that binds, reproduces, and preserves the person and the group. This kind of adaptation has been called by Professor Hugh Miller "associative adaptation."[3] The behavior of human beings is either "good" or "bad" to the extent that it is better or worse associatively adapted. "Associative adaptation" is here but another name for love. It is to be noted that it is not said that a person is either "good" or "bad," but that his behavior may be good or bad in virtue of its quality of associative adaptation or love. Our assumption has been throughout that all human beings (with a few possible exceptions) are basically good, but by unfortunate conditioning they are frequently caused to function badly. "Goodness," then, is virtually equatable with "love," and "badness" with a failure of love.

Ethics, then, for us becomes both the art and the science of the reciprocal adaptation of human beings to each other in love—in loving attitudes of mind and in loving conduct. There is, of course, nothing new in this view of ethical conduct. What is new is the scientific

[3] Hugh Miller, *Progress and Decline* (Los Angeles: Ward Ritchie Press, 1963); Hugh Miller, *The Community of Man* (New York: Macmillan, 1949).

validation which the discoveries made in recent years concerning the nature of human nature have brought to this view of ethics. Our revised conception of human nature, as set out in the pages of this book, should have the profoundest influence upon religion and ethics, but it should be fairly clear that religion and ethics are basically taught not so much in the churches as in the home and in the school. The churches should continue to develop and consolidate what has been taught in the home and in the school—if what has been there taught is sound and humane. If it is not, it does not seem to me that the church can do much to undo the damage that has been done. The churches should be the preservers not of inflexible orthodoxies but of the truths by which men must live and from which they must never depart— truths, however, which are infinitely perfectible. It is not with the institutionalization of the religious impulse, but with its education, that the church should be concerned, with the development of a religious attitude which embraces a sense of the possibilities of existence and a devotion to the cause of those possibilities. The church must become not merely the repository of the highest ideals of humanity, but an active participant in the educational process of helping human beings realize those ideals.

Christians believe that God is Love. Our inquiry in this book has amounted to the conclusion that Love is God. It is a distinction with a significance, the difference being that while most Christians accept the view that God is Love, and let it go at that, Jesus himself felt also that Love is God, that love of God was essential, but equally essential was the love of man for man. This seems to me to represent the great contribution of Jesus, the development of the seedling Old Testament injunction to love one's neighbor as oneself. Jesus not only sent men to God, but he also sent God to men, by sending men to men. He enjoined men to live a way of life with their fellow men which was the way of love—love for each other. This way of love I would call *philia,* distinguishing it from the Platonic and Old Testament "eros": love in which man seeks God in order to satisfy his spiritual hunger by the possession and enjoyment of the Divine perfection, and from the New Testament love of man for God, *agape,* which implies the whole-hearted surrender to God, placing one's entire faith in Him, and desiring only that His will should be done.

For too many modern Christians *agape* has taken the form of a kind of apple-polishing of the Divine. The concept of love which we have here been developing most closely resembles *philia,* but is not identical with it, for our concept is best called by what it refers to, namely, *maternal love.*

It will fall principally to mothers and teachers to spread this gospel, and toward this end I would strongly urge that the nursery school be made part of the educational system of the land. In nursery school children between two and five years of age would, for a few hours, each day receive the benefits of mother and teacher working together on the complementary task of contributing toward the child's development. The nursery school would represent the principal agency through which the parents could be brought together with the school in the complementary task of developing the potentialities of the child. In nursery school parents, especially the mother, would be encouraged to help teachers and teachers would be encouraged to help parents in the joint enterprise of helping the child. The parents would contribute what the teachers ought to know, and the teachers would contribute what the parents ought to know, for the benefit of the child as well as for the benefit of all concerned. The teaching the child receives at home and the teaching it receives at school must be joined and unified. The teaching of the elementary skills of reading, writing, and arithmetic is important, but not nearly as important as the most important of all the skills—human relations.

A scientific approach to education must begin with the basic assumption that values must in the long run be tested by their capacity to contribute to the happiness and creativeness of human beings living together. If we have found a scientific basis *in fact* for what *should be,* we should at least be willing to give it a try.

Our schools need to be transformed into institutes for the study of the science (theory) and the art (practice) of loving human relations. Children in such schools will continue to be taught the theory and practice of human relations from their earliest years. It is in the nursery, kindergarten, and elementary school that the most fundamental learning will be done, and it is for this reason that we must learn to understand that the most important teachers in the human community, in addition to the parents, are the teachers of the young. College professors in this scheme of values, valuable as they are, are not as important as elementary schoolteachers. Our society, therefore, needs to undergo a fundamental change in its attitudes toward schoolteachers, to revalue them for what they are worth—as next to the parents the most important members of the community, for teachers are the unacknowledged legislators of the world, the midwives of humanity. We need, therefore, to elevate the status and increase the prestige of the profession of teaching the young, and to reward its votaries in such a manner as to encourage the finest persons among us to dedicate their lives to the high and significant task of helping human beings realize their potentialities.

The teaching of the three "R's" must be secondary and supplementary to the teaching of the primary skill of human relations, for what, indeed, is any instruction worth if it is not integrated into an understanding of man's responsibility to man? Whatever is learned should be learned primarily with reference to its significance for human relations, and always with the emphasis on cooperation, on adaptive association, on love, on shared relationships. Cracker-barrel human relations are not good enough. Children should be taught not how to become submissive echoes of their teachers and their traditions, but how to evaluate humanely, sympathetically, and critically the world in which they are living. They should be taught not only the overt but also the covert values of their society, and they should be taught not only what is right with their society but what is wrong with it, and that it is going to be their responsibility to put things right, and how they may be put right.

In this light education must be conceived to be the development of the best that is within the person by making available to him all the encouragements and supports and stimulations that he requires, to enable him to become a loving, cooperative, nonconflictual person, who is not only aware of what is right with the world but is also equipped with the knowledge, the desire, and the wisdom necessary to bring it nearer that ideal of what it should and can be—a person who will not be a competitor, but a cooperator, a person for whom altruism will be a passion and selfishness a disorder; a person wise enough to know that

> He who would love his fellow men
> Must not expect too much of them . . .

a person who will want to improve the world as he finds it, and not accept things as they are; a person who will not risk wrecking the social machinery by exceeding the speed limit of rational inquiry; who will not abolish anything, but merely render it necessary to discontinue it, dispelling fear by supplying facts and knowledge; who will recognize the strange necessity of beauty; who will have a sense of personal responsibility for decency and justice; who will never offer up the smoke of incense before an empty shrine, nor pretend to a creed he does not believe; a person, in short, who having had a loving order made within himself will make loving order in the world—

be to other souls
The cup of strength in some great agony,
Enkindle generous ardour, feed pure love
Beget the smiles that have no cruelty—
Be the sweet presence of a good diffused,
And in diffusion more intense.

—GEORGE ELIOT

Survival and Fulfillment

Humanity today stands on the threshold of a possible new dispensation—the self-dispensing fulfillment of its evolutionary destiny. However, the struggle for survival, far from having diminished, has increased enormously, and for vastly greater numbers of human beings than ever before. Uncontrolled multiplication now threatens the continued existence of the species. Hunger and starvation, disease and despair now affect millions who should never have been born. We speak of life as sacred, but treat it as a thing that can be thrown away. The homily "The Lord will provide" is not true. Only humankind can provide. Quantity debases quality. Unless we solve the population problem at the individual level we shall be unable to solve any human problem. The stresses and strains of "civilized life" have become unbearable for masses of human beings. In the United States alone one out of every eighteen persons will spend some time in a mental hospital. Human survival should mean fulfillment of one's potentialities for being a loving, creative, cooperative human being. Julian Huxley has referred to this in the following words:

Human life *is* a struggle—against frustration, ignorance, suffering, evil, the maddening inertia of things in general; but it is also a struggle *for* something, and for something which our experience tells us can be achieved in some measure, even if we personally find ourselves debarred from any measure that seems just or reasonable. And fulfillment seems to describe better than any other single word the positive side of human development and human evolution—the realization of inherent capacities by the individual and of new possibilities by the race; the satisfaction of needs, spiritual as well as material; the emergence of new qualities of experience to be enjoyed; the building of personalities. But it cannot be achieved without struggle, not merely struggle with external obstacles, but with the enemies within our own selves.

The realization of inherent capacities by the person and of new possibilities by the race—that is what is meant by fulfillment. If human beings are enabled to fulfill themselves they will encounter no enemies within themselves. At the present time the greatest obstacle in the path of human progress is not the atom or hydrogen bomb or any other external obstacle, but in the disordered selves of human beings. The self of a human being is the means through which he sees and evaluates the world. An imperfect means applied to the achievement of confused goals is not the best of auguries for a happy dénouement. A self that is organized to function in acts of love is different in its effects from one that is disorganized to function on the dual basis of some sort of relation to society in which there is, first, a religion in some way concerned with the doctrine of love, and second, a secular tradition which offers high rewards to the successful competitor. Man requires no supernatural sanctions for love. Love is a fact of nature, and it is the most important of all the facts about human nature. Love is and should be the most natural of religions for human beings. The person who has been brought up to be a loving human being will not be able to see the world in anything but loving terms. Violence will be as foreign to his nature as it is at present common to the acquired nature of most men of contemporary Western civilizations. To most persons, conditioned as they are in the Western world today, love and violence are not only not incompatible but are perfectly reconcilable forms of conduct, whereas in fact violence is not only contrary to man's basic nature but inimical to it.

Man's self is the means of whatever ends he achieves, and the ends he seeks to achieve are largely determined by the nature of the self that has been built into him. Hence the pressing necessity of realizing that healthy human development and survival depends upon our ability to help human beings fulfill their potentialities and thus develop selves that are as much in harmony with their basic inner necessities as they are in harmony with those of all other healthy human beings. No man ever achieves his real self until he is his best self. We know something of the nature of those necessities, and we have good reason to believe that if we would but act upon that knowledge we will have taken the most important step in the right direction toward the fulfillment of humanity's promises.

Human nature is good. It is our present *human nurture* that is bad. We need to conform human nurture to the requirements of human nature. Our nurture must be based on basic human nature. Human beings and nations of human beings will solve their problems only when they have learned this lesson and applied it to themselves.

Truth is within ourselves; it takes no rise
From outward things, whate'er you may believe:
There is an inmost centre in us all,
Where truth abides in fulness; and around,
Wall within wall, the gross flesh hems it in,
Perfect and true perception—which is truth;
A baffling and perverting carnal mesh
Which blinds it, and makes error: and, *"to know"*
Rather consists in opening out a way
Whence the imprison'd splendour may dart forth,
Than in effecting entry for the light
Supposed to be without.
                              —BROWING, *Paracelsus*

ST. PAUL

•

On Love

St. Paul's description of love is both beautiful and sound.[1] In addition, it is quite astonishing, for it represents the first statement concerning the place and importance of love in the world of humanity. It is the teaching of Jesus presented in St. Paul's language. What a pity it is that so few Christians have understood its meaning.

I may speak in tongues of men or of angels, but if I am without love, I am a sounding gong or a clanging cymbal. I may have the gift of prophecy, and know every hidden truth; I may have faith strong enough to move mountains; but if I have no love, I am nothing. I may dole out all I possess, or even give my body to be burnt, but if I have no love, I am none the better.

Love is patient; love is kind and envies no one. Love is never boastful, nor conceited, nor rude; never selfish, not quick to take offence. Love keeps no score of wrongs; does not gloat over other men's sins, but delights in the truth. There is nothing love cannot face; there is no limit to its faith, its hope, and its endurance.

Love will never come to an end. Are there prophets? their work will be over. Are there tongues of ecstasy? they will cease. Is there knowledge? it will vanish away; for our knowledge and our prophecy alike are partial, and the partial vanishes when wholeness comes. When I was a child, my speech, my outlook, and my thoughts were all childish. When I grew up, I had finished with childish things. Now we see only puzzling reflections in a mirror, but then we shall see face to face. My knowledge now is partial; then it will be whole, like God's knowledge of me. In a word, there are three things that last for ever: faith, hope, and love; but the greatest of them all is love.

Put love first.

[1] I Corinthians 13, *The New English Bible*, 1970, p. 221.

For Further Reading

BAYLEY, JOHN, *The Characters of Love*. New York: Basic Books, 1960. The transformations of Eros, from the medieval romance to the modern novel.

BENOIT, HUBERT, *The Many Faces of Love*. New York: Pantheon Books, 1955. The psychology of the emotional and sexual life.

CAPELLANUS, ANDREAS, *The Art of Courtly Love*, transl. with an introduction and notes by John Jay Parry. New York: Columbia University Press, 1941. This is the classic work on courtly love written at the request of Marie de Champagne by her chaplain between the years 1184 and 1186.

D'ARCY, MARTIN C., *The Mind and Heart of Love*. New York: Henry Holt, 1956. Paperback: Meridian Books, 1956. In which it is brilliantly argued that Eros (human passion) and Agape (divine love) are quite reconcilable.

————, *The Meeting of Love and Knowledge*. New York: Harper & Row, 1957. As in the above work, this learned Catholic theologian and philosopher considers the relation of love to "the perennial wisdom."

DAY, DONALD, *The Evolution of Love*. New York: The Dial Press, 1954. An anthology of the evolution of love relations between the sexes.

FROMM, ERICH, *The Art of Loving*. New York: Harper & Row, 1956. A most helpful inquiry into the nature of love.

HUNT, MORTON M., *The Natural History of Love*. New York: Alfred A. Knopf, 1959. A history of emotional relationships between the sexes.

MONTAGU, ASHLEY, ED., *The Meaning of Love*. New York: The Julian Press, 1953. Ten distinguished contributors discuss the meaning of various aspects of love.

————, *The Direction of Human Development*. New York: Hawthorn Books, 1970. A detailed discussion of the biological and social bases of love.

NELSON, JOHN CHARLES, *Renaissance Theory of Love*. New York: Columbia University Press, 1958. Written around Giordano Bruno's *Eroici furori*.

NYGREN, ANDERS, *Agape and Eros*. London: S. P. C. K., 1953. Part I is devoted to a study of the Christian idea of love, and Part II to the history of the Christian idea of love.

REIK, THEODOR, *A Psychologist Looks at Love*. New York: Farrar & Rinehart Inc., 1944. A psychoanalyst's views of love.

DE ROUGEMONT, DENIS, *Love in the Western World.* New York: Pantheon Books, 1956. The historical paradox presented by the universal acceptance of marriage on the one hand, and on the other the enthralling attraction of romantic and passionate love outside marriage.

SCHNEIDER, ISIDOR, ED., *The World of Love,* 2 vols. New York: George Braziller, 1964. The best of all anthologies covering every aspect of love.

SOROKIN, PITIRIM A., ED. *Explorations in Altruistic Love and Behavior: A Symposium.* Boston: The Beacon Press, 1950. Seventeen leading authorities discuss various aspects of love.

SUTTIE, IAN D., *The Origins of Love and Hate.* New York: The Julian Press, 1952. A fundamental book on love and hate.

VALENCY, MAURICE, *In Praise of Love.* New York: Macmillan, 1958. A revealing study of the love poetry of the Renaissance.